'Oppression'

Ruby Langford Ginibi

My son's jail painting depicted:
Black hands tied together by white
chains, with blood running freely,
and our dreaming tracks underneath.
Can anyone explain? Why this violence
is directed at my people? The colonist
mentality still remains! And Koories are
still oppressed by the dominant society
of western laws, that the Westminster system
of justice brought with it over 200 years ago.
Black hands tied together by white chains,
blood running freely, and our dreaming tracks
underneath. This painting shows Jail, police Brutality,
deaths in custody, the lot. Can anyone explain, why
this convict mentality still remains?

April, 1993

Other books by Ruby Langford Ginibi

Don't Take Your Love to Town (1988)
Real Deadly (1992)
My Bundjalung People (1994)

HAUNTED BY
THE PAST

Ruby Langford Ginibi

ALLEN & UNWIN

First published in 1999 by
Allen & Unwin
9 Atchison Street, St Leonards 1590
Australia
Phone: (61 2) 8425 0100
Fax: (61 2) 9906 2218
E-mail: frontdesk@allen-unwin.com.au
Web: http://allen-unwin.com.au

National Library of Australia
Cataloguing-in-Publication entry:

Ginibi, Ruby Langford, 1934– .
  Haunted by the past.

  ISBN 1 86448 758 5.

  1. Aboriginal Australian prisoners—Biography. I. Title.

365.6092

Set in 11/13 pt Plantin Light by DOCUPRO, Sydney

10 9 8 7 6 5 4 3 2 1

I dedicate this book to my son Nobby and to every mother's son or daughter who has fallen foul of the Westminster system of justice that came with the first squatters and settlers in 1788. Those laws are not our Koori laws—our laws were the first laws of this land.

Since we Kooris are invaded people, we have always had to conform to other people's laws, rules and standards—we were never allowed to be ourselves as Aboriginal people.

Contents

Acknowledgements

To my son Nobby, who has given nineteen years of his life fighting, and surviving, in Her Majesty's Gaols in Australia; to Pam Johnston, for the report she wrote for Nobby's trial in 1987; to the *Daily Telegraph*, 21.6.73, 'The Breakout'; to the Committee to Defend Black Rights, for all the statistics and information on Aboriginal incarceration; to Helen Corbett for parts of her paper, read in Denmark, April–Sept. 1990 to The International Workgroup for Indigenous Affairs (I.W.G.I.A); to Jack Davis, for his poem 'John Pat'; to Robert Walker's mother, Linda, for his poem 'Solitary Confinement'; to Graham Dixon for his poem 'Battle Heroes'; to the *Encyclopedia of Aboriginal Australia* for the extract on David Gundy; to the Anti-Discrimination Board for information from their 1982 study of street offences by Aboriginals; to Arthur and Leila Murry; to my editor and dear friend, Penny van Toorn, without whose commitment and dedication this book would not have been completed. I've initiated her to the role of 'my tita'. Thanks very much Penny; to (third report) 1995, Aboriginal Torres Strait Islander Social Justice Commissioner Michael Dodson, report covers 1.7.94 to 30.6.95; to David English for his help with the computer; to the Australia Council for the Arts for funding a Senior Fellowship; and to every mother's son or daughter who has run foul of the Westminster system of justice that the colonists brought with them in 1788.

Preface

Haunted by the Past is a story about jail, juvenile incarceration and institutionalisation, and Aboriginal deaths in custody, written from a Koori perspective.

Though several articles and essays have been written about Aboriginal deaths in custody, one book that I helped launch is entitled *Voices of Aboriginal Australia: Past, Present and Future*, Butterfly Books, 1995. It was compiled by Irene Mores, an elderly white woman, and the Aboriginal Deaths in Custody Watch Committee: Arthur Murry, Marie Carter, Ray Jackson and Roderick Pitty.

In all, 99 cases of Aboriginal deaths were referred to the Royal Commission. This covered the period 1980–89. Not a single criminal charge was laid despite the most damning evidence. By 1994, after the death of Daniel Yock, there had been 151 Aboriginal deaths in custody since 1980. The recommendations of the Royal Commission have never been acted on properly.

The intensive police surveillance and harassment which culminated in Daniel Yock's death is part of an escalating pattern of police repression in working class areas: police officers follow and harass the youth, eventually provoking a reaction, then, according to one ex-police officer, make arrests on trumped-up charges. The charges—offensive language, resisting arrest, and obstructing police—are so common that they are known within the police force as 'ham, cheese and tomato'.

Why is this still happening in the 1990s? We've had the Royal Commission into Black Deaths in Custody and the Human Rights Commission Report into Racial Violence. In 1991, Human Rights Commissioners Irene Moss and Ron Costan, QC, found that relations between Aboriginals and police had reached crisis point because of widespread involvement of police in acts of violence, intimidation, and harassment. They found that racist attitudes and practices, both conscious and unconscious, were endemic and nation wide.

The Anti-Discrimination Board has come to similar conclusions. The board believes that some of the tension between the police and Aborigines is created and reinforced by the lack of police knowledge about Aboriginal culture, and their failure to appreciate it as a valid minority culture. There is constant labelling of Aborigines by police (and others) as drunks, lazy bludgers, thieves, and so on. This indicates a real failure to appreciate and understand the pressures and realities of the day-to-day existence of Aborigines; they have been dispossessed of their land, had their traditional lifestyle destroyed, and no meaningful replacement offered to them. They confront racial discrimination daily, and are denied the possibility of an independent economic existence developed on their own terms. In their study of 'street offences' by Aborigines in NSW country towns, the Anti-Discrimination Board recommended education programs for police, magistrates, judges, and people serving on juries, as they had little understanding of Aboriginal culture and the history of dispossession which forms the basis of many present-day problems.

Who could forget the TV footage of the policemen in Bourke in 1989 going to a fancy dress party with their skin blackened and nooses around their necks? A home video, screened on national TV in 1992, showed them pulling the nooses, gagging, and saying 'I'm David Gundy', 'I'm Lloyd Boney.' They thought this was a great laugh.

But Aboriginal people have worked hard to bring about changes for the better. Helen Boyle and Rose Stack, Aboriginal women living in Sydney, set up a Committee to Defend Black Rights (CDBR) after the acquittal of the five cops charged with the manslaughter of John Pat in 1983. At their meetings at Tranby College, the CDBR took up other cases where black deaths had occurred in custody under suspicious circumstances. They also campaigned to hold the Royal Commission into Black Deaths in Custody.

In 1987, Helen Corbett (nee Boyle), then National Chairperson of the CDBR, told the United Nations about Aboriginal deaths in custody. Such deaths are a breach of the United National International Covenant on Civil and Political Rights, to which Australia is a signatory, and is thus legally obliged to observe. Helen Corbett told the UN that one of our people died in custody, on average, every eleven days. She said we were the world's most imprisoned group of people—a fact which government reports themselves acknowledge. The figures she presented to the UN in 1987 showed that although we make up only 1.6% of the total Australian population, we comprise nearly 30% of all those in custody. Almost two-thirds of those jailings are for street offences such as 'drunkenness' and 'disorderly behaviour'. Two days after she delivered this address, the Federal Government established the Royal Commission into Black Deaths in Custody.

Helen Corbett went back to the UN two years later, in 1989. By that time another 32 Aboriginal people had died in custody. She calculated that the rate of Aboriginal deaths was proportionally equivalent to 2562 non-Aboriginal people dying in custody. She said that the Royal Commission had been established without negotiating the real issues with Aboriginal people; it had been set up out of political expediency, and had served as a way of pacifying criticism against the government during the bicentenary celebrations of 1988.

I was thinkin—all this bloody strugglin overseas for our rights. Wasn't anybody in Australia listening? Or, much less, caring?

Thirty million dollars were spent on that Royal Commission. But no fault was found. No charges were laid. Ninety-nine deaths were investigated, but not one police officer or prison officer or superintendent was found guilty of anything. Three hundred and thirty-nine recommendations were made, but it seems no one's bothered to implement them. Two of the main recommendations were that drunkenness should be decriminalised, and jailing should be absolutely the last resort for our young people. But these two simple steps to reduce the jailings and the deaths have not been taken.

Nationally, between 1989 and 1995, there were over 90 additional Aboriginal deaths in custody. New South Wales has the worst record, with a 113% increase in the Aboriginal prison population, and a 55% increase in the rate of Aboriginal deaths in prison just between 1994 and 1995.

Statistics from the New South Wales Department of Corrective Services show a steady growth in the average numbers of Aborigines serving full-time prison sentences in New South Wales—from 8.5% in 1987 to 14.2% in 1997. Aborigines make up less than 2% of the population.

Aboriginal kids aged 10 to 17, nationally in 1996, were 20 times more likely than other kids to be imprisoned. (In Queensland, they are 41 times more likely; in Western Australia, 31 times.) Aboriginal kids are more likely to be arrested than receive a summons; more likely to be refused bail; less likely to receive a caution; and more likely to receive a detention order.

So the rate Aboriginal people, and our kids especially,

are being imprisoned and dying in custody is still rising today. The killing times are not over. They're still goin on today. Big shame Australia, I say, big shame!

In the Menzies era, there was a very racist White Australia Policy, where no one with a black skin could come and live in Australia. They could come to study at the universities but, when their visas expired, they had to go back where they came from. Australia has since adopted 'multiculturalism' right over our Koori heads like we were never ever here, and the country was really *terra nullius*, the land of no one, which was a great lie. Instead of creating government policies to educate, house, and assist us Kooris to take our rightful place in Australian society, the governments of the past and present have always had a separatist policy which has excluded us from their mainstream society, and that exclusion is still in practice today—1998. Our dispossession and oppression stems from colonisation. What is colonisation? It is the power and dominance of one society over another.

Juvenile Justice—3rd report 1995
From Aboriginal and Torres Strait Islander Social Justice Commissioner Michael Dodson (this report covers from 1/7/94–30/6/95)
A now-deceased elder from one of the Kimberley communities, Western Australia, explained his people's view of the learning process. He drew a small spiral in the sand that represented the mother's womb.

> When you emerge from the womb you start learning; learning how to suck the mother's breast, how to hunt and so on. As you learn more, your spiral gets bigger. Aboriginal law kept people moving further out on that spiral. The more law you can learn, the richer your life

gets and the bigger the spiral, and the closer your link with the land.

The truth is that the spiral of young life is diminished by contact with the juvenile justice system. Traditional Aboriginal law grows up responsible young women and men who value and are valued by their communities. By contrast, the Australian juvenile justice system is a crude system of prohibitions and punishments.

Beneath the rhetoric of 'rehabilitation', carried out in correctional centres, lies the reality of a system that most often deepens the damage to kids who are already in trouble. This is so for all kids. But it has a particular impact on indigenous kids who are being drawn into custody at a phenomenal rate. At any one time, roughly 30% of the 'clients' at Minda Juvenile Justice Centre in Sydney are Aboriginal kids between the ages of 10 and 17 years. Our kids represent less than 1.9% of the juvenile population of New South Wales.

This gross over-representation in the youth prison population is not peculiar to New South Wales. Nationally, Aboriginal and Torres Strait Islander kids between the ages of 10 and 17 years are 18.6 times more likely to be held in detention than other kids.

Introduction
Pam Johnston

Nobby Langford's life experience has been as an alien in his own country. Nobby Langford is a descendant of the Bundjalung people from the Northern Rivers of the North Coast of New South Wales and Queensland. Bundjalung people are of matriarchal lineage. His tribal connection is directly through his mother. He is related by totem to a particular bird, Willy Wagtail, and knows much of the Bundjalung language. Although this knowledge has been with him much of his life, it has meant only a rejection from mainstream society. Nobby Langford comes from a nation within a nation!

Although he has a white father, he has been raised as a Koori. His whole life experience has been living on the fringe of society. As an Aboriginal his identity has been constantly denied. He is what is called a 'light' Koori. Society has offered him no place in which he sees he can fit, because Aboriginal people have no place in the dominant society of Australia. His boyhood was spent doing what his mother calls 'gut-breaking work' fencing in outback New South Wales and Queensland. Watching his mother struggle to raise nine children while their various fathers drank, and beat her, did not offer him a strong role model on which to build his life. He has a close and loving family despite its misfortunes, thanks to his mother's efforts. However the reality of the day-to-day struggle to exist, which was constantly reduced to not knowing where the next meal was coming from, was a nightmare. The family moved from place to place, not because they were an unreliable or unstable unit, but because the experience of being Aboriginal meant that they were subject to racism and prejudice hour by hour, according to how white society was feeling at that time. On the one hand there has always been a stereotype of an Aboriginal person that is so strong that one really has to fight it not to fall under its spell. On the other hand, what is an Aboriginal?

Nobby has stated often enough that he is a black man wrapped up in a white skin, so he's never been accepted into the white world because of his Aboriginal background, and not accepted in the black world because of his fair skin!

He was always pulled in different directions—the black way or the white way—it was very confusing to him. All his life the only reality was his Aboriginality because of being raised by a black mother, not by the white father!

The stereotype of an Aboriginal is that they are full-blooded with black, curly or frizzy hair, drunken, loud-mouthed bludgers! Welfare dependants, lazy layabouts, drunken boozers. White Australian society sees a drunken Aboriginal sauntering down the street, then they say, 'Oh, they are all like that!' But they never see our dispossession and our social non-acceptance as the cause of our drunkenness! They don't take the blame for any of the social disadvantages they have forced us to try and overcome!

In Nobby Langford's experience, being Aboriginal simply meant much pain and suffering, and despair. It meant discrimination and humiliation. It meant never having a safe place spiritually or physically.

This has been Nobby Langford's reality. Like many of our people he internalises his feelings. When the pressure gets too great, he hits back in an orgy of despair. This has

Introduction

been the only language given him, and thus the only one he knows. His experience in life is that his history and identity have been denied. He sees this as not only his own experience, but that of all Aboriginal people. Where then could you say there was hope and justice in his life? The only real joy was family and, in a very short space of time, he lost not one, but two beloved brothers as well as his older sister. He was suddenly the eldest male in the family. In this period he also lost a loved uncle, his mother's brother, a great-aunt, and his grandmother. This series of blows was more than the family could humanly endure, and certainly more than Nobby Langford could, as his history shows. The start of these series of family deaths coincides with the start of his trouble with the law. His boyhood was lost to back-breaking work and fringe dwelling. His youth was spent in grief, and irrational and desperate acts—hitting back at a society that showed it did not care for him or his people. His manhood has been spent in trying to fit into a society that he cannot fit into because he is Aboriginal. This is not an uncommon story among Aboriginal people. This is not about a man who has an unreasonable chip on his shoulder. Nobby Langford is the living product of Aboriginal history.

What has been written about Nobby Langford in terms of his criminal record has been from a whiteman's view. It is said again and again that the difference between reading these arrest sheets and then actually meeting the person referred to is extraordinary! He is a sensitive, articulate, and intelligent human being. His formal education is minimal, but he presents as a very educated man. Where is the reality?

A few years ago, Nobby started painting and exploring his Aboriginal spirituality in order to discover more about himself, and has developed himself as an urban Koori artist of considerable significance. His paintings are exciting, and are drawing much comment in the artistic community, nationally and internationally. His lifelong identity crisis in terms of his alienation from white society is now being resolved through his Aboriginal art. The fact that this—and therefore he himself—has a significant place in the world is important. Throughout the world, art tells us who we are, as much as it inspires the human spirit to be grand.

Nobby Langford is constantly seeking knowledge of his own culture as something that belongs to him, and was stolen from him. In his community, he also has a role as an older man in relation to young men around him, and he was clearly taking this role very seriously in jail. Because he is able to read and write, something he taught himself over the years, and is reasonably articulate, he has been able to assist other Aboriginal men with their legal problems. He also regularly assisted in communication with home and family through writing letters on behalf of the illiterate. He encouraged other Aboriginal inmates to paint, and passed on what knowledge he had. This was fairly difficult in prison as the active policy of prison administration is to discourage racial grouping, although the nature and culture of Aboriginal people is communal.

What does all this mean? It means that Nobby Langford has now found a direction and place based on what he is—an Aboriginal person. He no longer needs to hit out and react in a negative way. He has taken charge of who he is, and how he defines himself, based on the truth of Aboriginal people and Aboriginal ways. Nobby Langford's self-esteem can only grow with the knowledge and education he gains. He stands before you in this book as an Aboriginal person, a descendant of the Bundjalung people, and he must be seen according to that reality. He is not a white person and never has been; he must not be seen through white eyes.

People say Australia is not like Chile or Argentina or

South Africa. They say that we are more civilised. We Aboriginal people wonder about that as we look at what has been done in our land and to our own people by civilised nations. Nobby Langford has lived this history. We always hope for justice and even now as you read his story, we hope that he will be seen and considered for what he is—a Bundjalung man whose boyhood, youth, and early manhood have been stolen from him by the oppressor nation. He deserves hope in his life, and he has given himself a reason for living through his art and culture. Nobby Langford has not only shown potential as an Aboriginal artist, he is well on the way to developing an exciting and significant career as an Artist. Nobby Langford is a man from a different culture—a culture which is alien to police and courts and prisons. He comes from a culture that has been shown, historically and currently, to have every reason to fear 'whiteman's justice' and to expect nothing of it. Despite this, he has shown himself to be a man who can rise from the ashes of his life and do something with it!

With all hope for justice,

Pam Johnston, M.A., PhD
Boomalli Aboriginal artist; Aboriginal Art and Culture teacher, Long Bay Gaol; Aboriginal Studies lecturer at City Art Institute; teacher and PhD, Creative Arts, University of Wollongong.

1

BEGINNINGS

When does Nobby's story begin? With his birth in 1955?
Or further back, with my struggle as an Aboriginal woman
raising nine children mostly on my own? Or maybe
Nobby's story starts even earlier than that in the 1880s,
when my family went to live on Box Ridge Mission after
their traditional lands were taken over by the first squatters
up in the north of New South Wales. Thinking about it,
I'd say Nobby's story has its roots way back. It's part of a
bigger historical picture and a longer story of hardships
passed down from one generation to another. This story
continues today.

I was born on Box Ridge Mission at Coraki in 1934.
I think it was called that name because of all the box trees
growin there; it was good burnin wood for the old fuel
stoves and open fireplaces we had.

When that mission kicked off, there were only three
Koori families there. There were the Yukes, the Wilsons,
and the Andersons. My grandfather was Sam Anderson.
He came from across the Queensland border, from a place
called Boona, near Beaudesert. He was from the Wakka-
wakka clan of the Bundjalung tribes, and he married my
Gummy Mabel Yuke. My grandparents had seven children—four boys and three girls. My father, Henry, was the

1

eldest, then there was Bob, young Sam, and Gordon, who died young, aged thirteen, by drowning in the river at Kyogle on the Stoney Gully Mission.

Aunt Kate Anderson married Uncle Christie Bolt of Cabbage Tree Island. They had nine children. Aunt Kate died young. Three of their children and Uncle Chris are deceased. Aunt Eileen Anderson married Uncle James Morgan who became the first full-blood member appointed to that infamous 1964 Aboriginal Protection Board. He also spoke twelve of the dialects of the Bundjalung National. He died on National Aborigines Day celebration in Casino in 1968, aged 65. They had seven children, four of them now deceased. Aunt Phyllis, the youngest, had only one child, Julie, who was born in 1955, the same year as Nobby.

I remember my Auntie Eileen tellin me that when she was a little kid, they lived in bark humpies. There were no real homes, and Box Ridge was situated right next to the cemetery at Coraki. Years later Box Ridge was referred to as a cemetery because it was a place of death and destruction. Lots of children died because of poor health facilities. So did adult Kooris too.

As the family grew up they all branched out in search of work. They went from one mission to another. Some went to Cabbage Tree Island, some to Stoney Gully Mission in Kyogle, some to Tabalum, where that old mission was called Gulingarnullingee which means 'listen to the voice of the people'.

No matter where I go, my thoughts always go back to the mission where I was born. It seems to draw me back like a magnet. I remember the old missionary who used to come in a sulky each Sunday.

The Protection Board had sent Christian missionaries in since the 1890s because the full-blooded tribal people were regarded as heathens—without a god. What they never understood, those missionaries, was that our people already had their own religion. Our Dreaming stories say that before creation times, when the earth was flat, the great spirit forces moved over the land creating the mountains, the valleys, the rivers and streams, and everything that is in them. Aboriginal people were animals, birds, fish, insects, before we became human beings. We are a totemic people, and believe that when we die we are reincarnated as those totems. That is our belief, and it's as relevant as any other concept of creation and religion.

Born-again, or Pentecostal, Christians are Christians who have forgotten about Christian ways, then found them again. My people forgot their spiritual beliefs and adopted the missionaries' beliefs. Our spiritual beliefs are identical to the missionaries' beliefs anyway, but they denied us our Aboriginal culture, spirituality, and heritage.

Anyway, those missionaries did a pretty good job of Christianising my people, because every time I go there, I can see that they're all born-again Christians.

I remember back to when I was a child, how they would hold meetings at different homes during the week. They were Christian meetings. A whole set of people showed up and sat on the verandahs. There was always music—guitars, harps, mouth organs, and spoons. I can remember one old bloke playin the jew's harp. The sound intrigued me and the other kids—the twang twang twang blendin in with all the other instruments. It made for good listenin but the songs were all hymns. Us little ones sat quietly enjoying the music and singin.

Guinea fowls ran around everywhere. These speckled fowls' loud calls—KAH KAH KAH—echoed all around the mission, sometimes frightenin us little kids. While we were on the mission and Dad was in the bush workin as a log-cutter and carter, Mum ran away and left us. Ted Breckenridge and Lucy were the old couple whose house we lived in on Coraki mission. Old Ted made millett brooms in the back shed. He had about an acre of millett growin on the mission. I couldn't understand how this old black man learnt how to make them. Probably some white man taught him. I was six at the time, and Gwenny was four, and Rita was the baby, only two years old. Some of the old ones got word to Dad and he took us out in the bush with him and Uncle Ernie Ord. If he hadn't done that, we would've been taken away by the Protection Board. Living with Dad in the bush, that was how me and my sisters escaped being part of the Stolen Generation.

While Dad cut the trees, Old Uncle Ernie Ord looked after us in a little bush camp. Uncle Ernie used to take us huntin for bush tucker, and I never realised that all he was tellin us, with the stories and all, was his way of handin on to us kids our history and culture and heritage.

Uncle Ernie Ord used to tell us about bunihny (por-cupine), bingingh (turtle), burbi (koala), and the story about the frilly neck lizard who was a young boy who wouldn't listen to what the elders told him, so one night, when he was sleeping, the elders turned him into a frilly neck lizard with scaly skin and big floppy ears. When he asked the elders why he had scaly skin and big ears, the elders told him, 'You have those big ears so you will listen to what we are telling you now!' And the story of the brolga, that he was a very promiscuous bird running around after all the lady brolgas, and he wouldn't stop when the elders told him, so the elders hit him on the head with the digging sticks. And that's why the brolga has a red patch on his head, that's the blood and he was never promiscuous again. He only takes one partner for life, and only dances for her.

All the lessons of life about carin and sharin and loving each other is what was handed on to us, and how to get bushtucker, geebungs, bunyanuts, how to dig for yams. He

4

was a cleverman—a we-un-gali—a tribal doctor, though I didn't understand this when I was little. All the knowledge he was passin on to me has come in good stead. It has enriched my life and shown me who and what I am—an Aboriginal person.

Uncle Ernie used to make ashes damper, and kill goannas and roast them on the hot coals. He robbed swans' nests for eggs for us kids; half of one egg was sufficient, as they were too big for us little kids. He also cooked johnny cakes and my dad made the sweets. It was a jam roly-poly made up of scone dough rolled out flat with heaps of jam spread on it, then rolled up in a pudding cloth and placed in boiling water until cooked. Then he'd make custard and pour it over—Mmmm—sure tasted good as I remember. We collected berries too—lilli pilli, wild cherries, and guavas grew wild everywhere, so we never went without. The farmers around there used to grow corn for stock food, but they'd give us some if we asked them. Uncle Ernie would cook it up in the same water as the corned beef was cooked in. It was beautiful. We went fishin too when we were near the old Richmond River. There were mullet and garfish, and cobra worms from the rotted willow wood in the river. Sometimes there was catfish too, and jewfish. The Richmond River ran into the ocean at Ballina, and sometimes sharks came upriver to feed followin the schools of mullet. They were exciting times when the mullet were runnin. All the mission people would be there at the riverbank, fishing, and the cooking fires would be burning brightly in the old shacks on the mission. They seemed to lift everyone's spirits for a while. The men from the mission still went huntin bush tucker to supplement the old rations that Mrs Hiscocks handed out each month (which didn't last long at all).

Mrs Hiscocks was the mission manager when I was a kid. Later, she became the matron of that infamous

Cootamundra Girls' Training Home where they trained the stolen children to be serviced out as slaves, which ended up with a national inquiry that John Howard has never apologised for. He gets gagged on the word 'Sorry'. This National Report was tabled in parliament in April 1997 and made Kim Beazley, the leader of the opposition, cry. The report, titled *Bringing Them Home*, states:

> We may go home, but we cannot relive our childhoods. We may reunite with our mothers, fathers, sisters, brothers, aunties, uncles, communities, but we cannot relive the 20, 30, 40 years that we spent without their love and care, and they cannot undo the grief and mourning they felt when we were separated from them. We can go home to ourselves as Aboriginals, but this does not erase the attacks inflicted on our hearts, minds, bodies and souls, by caretakers who thought their mission in life was to eliminate us as Aboriginals.[1]

Even today, people like the matron Mrs Hiscocks do not take responsibility for what they did to our Aboriginal people, as they state 'they were only doing their jobs'.

Times were hard on the mission in the 1930s but at least we had each other. We had family units which clung together and helped each other and lived together. Us kids knew who we were and where we belonged.

After a while, I went to Bonalbo to live with Dad's brother and sister-in-law. When I was fifteen, Dad brought me to Sydney so Gwen could finish her schooling and I could find work. I went into the rag trade and became a machinist.

That move to Sydney alienated us from our family, our kith and kin and country. From that time I was no longer protected by my Bundjalung family's community. When I was seventeen I had my first child. I had four de facto unions—two with Aboriginal men and two with white men, one of whom I married. So I know what it's like in both worlds. I made my mistakes and buried my dead and I fell whichever way life hit me. But I always bounced back because I'm not a quitter and I survived, and am still survivin!

But back then I grew up and went out into the big wide world to find my own way. I moved around rural New South Wales and Queensland. The men came and went; the babies came and stayed. And they're still here, grown up today, although three are gone into the spirit world. I now have 21 grandchildren and three great-grand-children.

I didn't go back to my tribal country for 48 years. I was very unprotected, living like I was tribal but with no tribe around me. The term, 'living like I was tribal' means living like we did for centuries before the white man came, hunting bush tucker, gathering food. Today in Australia, there are three types of Aboriginal people: the traditional (full-blood) ones, out in the desert sitting on a rock with a spear in his hand; the mission-bred Kooris like me; and the urban Kooris around the cities and townships. But we are all one mob, only from different tribal areas. Like many of my people I travelled around from one place to another, like my ancestors, but I lived worse off than the poorest of poor whites. We were fringe dwellers, shantytown people in our own country. And there was no family around me to teach my kids their Aboriginal heritage.

This is the world I brought Nobby into, along with his brothers and sisters.

2

MY JARJUM

My son Nobby was born on 21 May 1955, at what was then the Newtown Women's Hospital. It was one of the first hospitals that cared for unmarried girls who were awaiting the births of their babies, though I did not identify as an unmarried mother. I took the name of his father— Mrs Campbell, I was known as then.

At the time of his birth, me and his father, and my three other children, Pearl (three), Billy (four) and Dianne (one), were living in Great Buckingham Street, Redfern, in a one-room flat that my dad had found for us when we came back to Sydney from Toowoomba in Queensland, in 1954. Each week, when I went to have my checkups, I'd catch a train to Newtown station and walk to the hospital.

Nobby was born sucking his fist! And he was the biggest baby I ever gave birth to. I remember the sister who was assisting the doctor in the birth wrapping my baby son up in a cloth, saying, 'I've gotta weigh this one. Look how big he is!' And she took off for the next room, then came back in to me saying, 'He's 9 lb 15 oz. You just missed the 10 lb number by one ounce.' So he was a *big* baby, and very fair, like his father.

At the time of his birth, Nobby's father Gordon thought that Nobby was the apple of his eye, being his first-born child ever! He checked him out to see if he had blue eyes like him, and was disappointed to see Nobby's eyes were brown like mine, but Nobby had his fair skin so I reckon that compensated for the lack of blue eyes. We were together for five years, and he fathered two more of my children, David and Aileen, and never showed much love or affection to the kids anyway. And he never stayed around after our union broke up. So he was not there to raise Nobby, David or Aileen. That job was left to me.

I gave my baby son the nickname 'Nobby' because if a boy baby cried too much, or his navel cord wasn't tied correctly, it caused a lump on the navel to stick out like a rupture. In those days, the old remedy for this was to poke cotton wool into the navel, then push it in and place a penny over the top of it, and stick it down with sticking-plaster. Nobby's navel did grow back in as he grew, so those old remedies really worked, but I'm afraid his nick-name of 'Nobby' stuck to him all his life.

After Nobby was born we moved to Coonabarabran. We were taking a friend there, and the car broke down so we were stranded there with only the clothes we were wearing. We had to take a job of 'burning off' because we had no money to pay for the car part we ordered. The boss advanced us the money to fix the car, so we could go out the four miles on Purlewah Road to do the work. We slept in the car, a box Plymouth it was, kept our food box in a tree, drank water from the creek, and the boss supplied a 'killer' (sheep) a week, which we killed and kept in a meat safe hung in the tree too!

I can remember the times when Nobby was a kid, and we lived in a tent on the Gunnedah Hill in Coonabarabran. I had four of my children born there in Coona.

Writing Nobby's story I wanted to include *his* recollections of the past. So we sat down together and I asked him, 'Tell me your memories of your childhood, son; what you remember of me draggin you around from pillar to post with the rest of the family. Don't feel you need to withhold anything.'

I remember livin in a tent. My last actual memory of bein a kid, was when my brother David and me hadn't seen our father for a long time, and he came and virtually left the same day and he left us something, a toy, a little gun that shot ping pong balls. David was on one side of the tent and I was on the other. We used to shoot these balls back and forward to each other.

I remember you carting water, Mum, in those four-gallon buckets on yokes you carried on your shoulder. Me and Billy would cart the wood you'd cut, in a billycart. And you were forever doin gut-bustin work. As far as us kids were concerned, you were the hardest workin mother in the world.

Once in Coonabarabran, when he was about two years old, I took him up town to shop, and later sat yarning with other Kooris under the shade of the tree guards, in the middle of the street. They asked me, 'Whose child you mindin?' And I snapped back, 'He's my son! No one else's.' And I walked away from them real insulted. But then I busted out laughing, cause I could see why they were askin me that because he was very fair, and had platinum blond hair. They'd thought he was a white kid, not mine!

Nobby was a normal kid, getting into mischief and mucking up in general. Sometimes he needed a good slap on the backside, which he *got* when he deserved it. He was the fairest of all the kids, but he always knew he was of Aboriginal descent! And with my close-knit little family he was never made to feel he was any different to the others. They were all one mob—sisters and brothers together to fight the world in this divided society we live in.

My Jarjum

I remember roughly goin to school. We used to catch a bus down the foot of the mission. It was a pretty good time. It was hard, but good. Us kids and the family had nothin, but we were happy.

I also remember a guy named Bobby Cameron. He used to get permission off Mum to take us kids on walkabout to the town dump in Coona to scratch around for toys and parts of old prams for billycarts and scooters. David and I once found an old box camera. We didn't know what it was at the time, but we kept clickin away, clickin away, till David said, 'Stop doin that, Nobby! You'll flatten the battery!'

I can't remember moving to Sydney when I was a kid. I think I was about seven or eight. All I remember is all us kids and Mum holdin up the train in Coona, because we didn't have the right fare, and Mum borrowed the rest off the taxi driver, Jacky Milligan. She give him her endowment book in payment, and he said he'd post it on to her, after he collected the money Mum owed him for our fares. Then we were on our way to the big smoke, as Mum called it.

When we came to Sydney from Coonabarabran, it was 1962. We moved from place to place, suburb to suburb, for nearly ten years. I dragged my kids from pillar to post—but I always managed to keep a roof over their heads.

Mum enrolled us in Cleveland Street School, and that's where I started to play football. Not long after, we moved again from Nanna Joyce's to Ann Street, Surry Hills. My recollection of Ann Street was it was a real big long street on a hill, and us kids used to make skateboards outa old rollerskates—take em apart, bash em with a hammer, and nail em onto a lump of wood, and go hurtlin down the hill. And we used to go to the soup kitchens. We used to get pies and sausage rolls at the Salvation Army place, have a feed and bring food home for

11

the rest of the family. We went to Prince Alfred Park to ice skate, when we could afford it.

I'm not quite sure how long we stayed at Ann Street, Surry Hills, but I can remember us all packin up and moving to Katoomba in the Blue Mountains somewhere in 1963 or '64. Up there in the Blue Mountains it was absolutely gorgeous. It was one of the happiest times of my life as a kid. The first year it snowed. We built a snowman, all us kids. Katoomba was real cold. But we had an open fireplace. Us kids used to go gather the wood with an old billycart. We had a few stray dogs around the place—Tiger an' Rin Tin Tin. And we had fruit trees in the backyard—pears, apples, and a plum tree outside the girls' bedroom winder. We also had a swing on a tree with a car tyre tied to it. The house was always full of kids—all annoying the shit outa Mum!

David and I had a fetish for coffee when we were kids. After Mum had done the shoppin, each fortnight I think it was, we used to sneak out into the kitchen in the middle of the night after everyone was asleep, and make a little pot of coffee. It was made with cold water, coffee, Sunshine powdered milk, and heaps of sugar. Delicious it was. One night we snuck out there. David was at the door watchin, while I made the coffee. Same little tin had the coffee in it, or so I thought. I put the sugar in and the coffee, and milk, and we sneaked back to our bedroom to drink it. But this night somebody—I don't know who it was but I tend to think it was Mum—had put chilli powder into the coffee tin. We didn't know where this coffee came from, but by god, it was hot! We just about drunk a bathful of cold water.

We went to Katoomba Primary School, where I started playin football again. By now, I really liked playin football. I also made it to the school swim team. All us kids were taught to swim by Mum, cause when she was young she was a pretty good swimmer. And it was sort of like you had to learn to swim. Did pretty well at it too, as I remember.

It was a big picnicking area, and we used to go to the Bridal Veil Falls at Leura. Used to be a little swimmin hole there too. All the family would go to enjoy the Three Sisters, the Jenolan Caves, and the Scenic Railway. We went virtually everywhere in Katoomba, we were locals up there then.

We had to climb a big hill to get to the main street. That hill was real steep, like 'heartbreak ridge'! There were about six million bloody steps to climb, and us kids spent most of the mornin runnin up and down those stairs on our way to school. Then we'd just about exhaust ourselves again comin back down in the afternoon. We were probably the fittest kids in the Blue Mountains.

I remember it just like it was yesterday, when there was just the three of us boys, the three musketeers—Billy, David, and me. We went nearly everywhere together as kids. We used to watch that TV show, 'Shintaro, the Samurai'. There was Tombey the mist, and the Coga Ninjas every afternoon on black and white TV. We'd get dressed up just like them bloody Ninjas. Shintaro was a Shogun or Samurai, and we used to make swords outa sticks and attack each other in the backyard. We'd jump up and down on stumps and chairs.

I remember us three walkin around lookin for something to do, sticks in hand, smashin rocks. We ended up at Catalina Raceway, and we were walkin around there, when we saw this big big black snake tryin to get up an embankment. It would've been about nine or ten feet long. Biggest snake I'd ever seen in m'life. If we'd a known then that it was tryin to get away from us, we wouldn't have annoyed the shit outa it, with sticks, and throwin stones at it. We were pokin it with a stick when a big huge man in a ranger's uniform come driving up in his land rover. When he jumped out, us kids shit ourselves, because he looked like the voice of authority—the coppers!

He yelled, 'What are you bloody kids doin?'

'Nothin mister.'

He coited us up the arse and gave us a lecture about how dangerous this snake was. Then he sent us on our way, and made sure we didn't come back.

As I said, we were poor but happy in Katoomba. At least that's how it seemed to me. This is why I've moved up there now—this is 1996. And I've always found the people in the mountains, or up and around that area, very kind and generous. Ya know, people saw Mum battling with us kids and always helped out. The cake shop was my favourite.

I think it was 1965 when we moved back to Sydney to Redfern. Mum tells me we stayed at her sister Margaret's place in Eveleigh Street, Redfern for about a year until we got the place at 2 Fitzroy Street, Newtown.

In Sydney was where all my troubles started. Bein poor— we had nothing—it was totally different from the Blue Mountains. But at Cleveland Street Primary I excelled in football. We would go to Victoria Park to play and meet up with other Koori kids.

I was about eleven years old then. It was like living in a ghetto, poverty all around us. If a person had a car and you didn't—it was a kind of status thing, and you'd go out and bloody well steal one. I had mates who used to steal cars, and wallets, and Christ knows what. And I came to be a part of that crowd. We were all about the same age, but these kids had been in Redfern longer than me, so they were the seasoned veterans.

Once ya hung around underprivileged kids you adopted a lot of their characteristics. They might steal a bottle of Coke out of a backyard or shop. Then it's your turn: 'I did it last week; you gotta do it this time!' So you go over a back fence in Newtown. I think we stole a bottle of drink outa nearly every bloody shop or milk bar in King Street Newtown! If anybody chased us, we'd scatter in all directions, run every which way. There'd be about twenty of us, so the shop keeper could only catch one, usually the littlest. Ross Wallace was the

smallest of our crew. So was David. Wayne Towney was also
very small. But all of us bigger guys—I was pretty tall for my
age—the shop keeper would give up on us.

I remember when we lived in 2 Fitzroy Street, Newtown,
in the sixties, Nob was running with a cool drink bottle
up the laneway near our place, when he tripped and fell
into the brick wall, breaking the bottle which cut him
deeply in the arm. I heard the crash and came running to
find him bleeding terribly. Some plumbers with a truck
wrapped his arm in a towel and rushed him to Prince
Alfred Hospital where they performed surgery to stitch his
sinews together. At first he couldn't move his fingers, but
later the surgeon gave him a rubber ball and paid him a
dollar a day to keep squeezing it to get the use back in his
fingers.

It was while we lived at Fitzroy Street that Owen
Mortimer, the English master, used to round up the two
eldest boys, Bill and Nobby, and take them to Kings'
School at Paramatta for the school holidays. He had a
program for underprivileged boys to go there to workshop
plays, do swimming and horse riding. Once he even took
the boys to Coffs Harbour because he had a brother who
had a banana plantation there. They came back with the
biggest banana bunch in the boot of the car. The kids had
bananas for quite a while.

As they were growing up, Nobby and David were both
in and out of trouble, in boys' homes for stealing, running
away from home, joyridin in hot cars. I think they were
twelve or thirteen years old then. I remember bringing
them home from one children's court and crying out loud.
Showing them my hands sayin, 'Look, no bloody policeman has ever fingerprinted these hands. But you two little
buggers have outdone me, ya mother.' I was so angry. I
threatened them with a good beltin when we got home.

When I was about twelve, I ran into Danny and Ken Weldon. There were six of us that used to hang around a lot together in Newtown. Because one of us got pinched for stealing something outa Coles, we all decided to run away. We were goin back to the bush. That day we never went back home after school. We had our little dilly-bags with us that we'd packed the day before, and we snuck down to the goods' rail. In those days the goods' train stopped at MacDonaldtown Station. It was gettin dark, and Philip and Ian Chattfield were with us too. We all jumped this goods' train, thinkin we were goin back to the bush. If I'd a known how dangerous it was, I would never have done it. On the train we kept gettin the black smoke from the old steam engine. We'd cough and spit and splutter, and we sometimes fell asleep because of the rattling of the train. We woke up and, Jesus, there were a lot of trees around. We must be gettin out into the real bush now! But then we stopped and a railways guard come strollin up and down the train. He was probably checkin the wheels, but back then, we were sure he was after us. So we all jumped off the train and scampered down the road. We came across a waterhole and decided to go for a swim. We loved being back in the scrub. But then we got grabbed by the coppers, or maybe they were railway guards. It turned out we were only in Liverpool, and we were swimmin in the town's water supply. So we were marched back home to Newtown, and Mum give us all a real earful. Ross, David, Wayne, Joe, Danny, Kenny, Ian and Philip—I haven't seen any of those guys for about twenty years; they were our little gang.

We went to the Foundation for Aboriginals in George Street in the sixties on Friday and Saturday, to the dances. There was no drinkin then, but bein the ratbag kids we were, we'd round up our pennies, and threepences and sixpences, and get one of the old fellas we knew to get us a bottle of brown muscat. Two of the little caps full of the muscat each, and you'd have ten or twelve kids wobblin all over the bloody place. We'd get real cheeky and go pickin fights with different little gangs. Prince Alfred ice skating gang used to punch on with us all the time.

This same crew that I grew up with, we all went through the boys' home ranks together, had the same girlfriends, same fashions of dressing. Those days we were sharpies, 'sharpie shit' they called us—crew-cut hairstyle, no sox, crestneck sweaters, high-waisted pants and driver shoes. We were supposed to strut around like king shits. We stole a bus in Newtown once, but it wasn't me, terrorising through the streets of Newtown, pickin up sheilas that we knew. It was a bit of a crazy time bein a sharpie.

I soon grew out of that. Then the skinheads came into it. We sharpies were not like the skinheads, those bastards threw people off trains, attacked old women on trains, punched the shit outa pensioners, and because sharpies had crewcut hairstyles like the skinheads, coppers naturally assumed we were like them too, but there was a difference. They wore hob-nail boots and big black straps around their necks. Brutal they were, and that was my sharpie days in the sixties.

I used to go to John Henry's, like Billy, my eldest brother. It was a night spot for sharpies. Billy could fight like Tyson and, because I was Bill's younger brother, a lot of the dudes on the door would let me in. They feared Billy, and probably thought I'd be running up to Bill to dob em if they never let me in. He'd sure sort em out. I had girlfriends here and there. It was like I always had a place to go. Once people knew how good my brother could fight, they'd think, 'God, if Bill can fight like that, he must have taught his younger brother.' David also ended up bein a boxer. I mainly played football, and Billy liked soccer. He did weights. He was full on with sports, I suppose I got off on my brother's thunder or his credibility, his glory.

Billy went to Newtown Boys' High, and his little brother went there too, a coupla years later. At high school I had virtually the same mates or cronies that I'd always knocked around with, but I picked up a few more on the way.

There were only seven Kooris in that whole school, out of six or seven hundred students. Us blackfellas, we hung out together. At first a lot of the other students didn't realise I was a blackfella because I had fair skin. But they soon got the picture once they knew I was Billy's brother, and that I talked like a blackfella, acted like a blackfella, and was as poor as a blackfella could ever be. Us Kooris all just knocked around together. We watched each other's backs, and it's basically the same when you go to jail.

At high school in those days, ya know the best fighter was the best liked. But when I went to high school after being in primary, I was following in my brother's footsteps. Him bein the knuckler that he was, it turned out that when I came to Newtown High, I copped all the shit he used to give out. I used to come home with black eyes and bruises and busted lips. One day when I come home, Bill said to me, 'What's goin on, Nobby?' I stuck staunch and wouldn't tell him but later he got it outa me. Bill had left school by that time so he wasn't there to protect me. When I told him what was happenin, he said, 'When ya go back to school, you offer out the three biggest bastards and tell them you wanta see them in the lane after school. Tell em you'll fight them one out.'

The little lane over from the school was a dead end where kids used to sort out their differences after school—all these little gangs, or else fighting one on one, just having a punch up, ya know. Anyway, I've come to school, and said to the three biggest blokes 'I'm gonna punch ya lights out after school. I'll see yous in the lane after school.' Nobody knows how much fear I went through sayin that to them big blokes. They were like monsters to me. I was literally lookin up to them. As the day was goin past I was bitin my nails. I was shitting meself. And I sure was hoping Bill would make it in time.

I come outa the school, and they're waitin for me at the

gate sayin, 'We're gonna kick the livin shit outa you, ya black bastard, ya little piece of garbage.' So I march into the lane beside them. Then they all stand behind me so I can't get out. They're facing me. They're takin off their shirts, ready to kick the livin daylights outa me.

Then my knight in shining armour turned up—on a red pushbike, not a white horse. Bill was workin as a telegram boy. As he put his bike on the ground, they heard him come up, and turned around, and if a white person can go whiter than they already are, I saw three white sheets standing in front of me. Bill walked up and said, 'I hear you blokes've been givin my young brother a hard time.'

By this time there was a crowd there, about twenty kids, girls and boys, because Enmore Girls' High was just up the corner. My big brother was taunting the three big blokes into a scrap. I knew he'd win cause he was awesome in a fight. I'm standin there, goin silly, mouthin off, and fuming with bravado. Then my shirt come off and Bill's shirt come off. He deadset wiped the floor with two of them; the third he left for me.

This bloke give me a serve first, but in the end I got over him because I had big brother there eggin me on, sayin, 'Don't you ever let these bastards beat you up ever again!' It's what sustained me, so I chopped in and kicked the livin shit outa this bloke. All my mates that I grew up with saw how ferocious I was in a scrap. It probably had a lot to do with my brother being there as he was the king of the heap!

I came to school next day, walkin tall, chest stuck out. After that I had no dramas with prefects. Everyone just left me alone. I've got my brother Billy to thank for that. Even though I'm fair and he's real dark, he acknowledged the fact that I was his brother! Because I'm fair I live ninety per cent of my life in a sort of divided culture. Some Kooris say, 'You don't look like a blackfella!' But that's not my fault. I've got a black mother; I can't help it if my father is white! It's something I've had to live with all my life.

The teachers were not racist, least I never ran into any racism, I think because of the fact that I was fair skinned, and I was a big kid. Soon as any sport teacher saw me, they asked, 'Can you play football?' Being a kid—like all kids are shy, when they're put in a spot—I would just nod my head. 'Well,' the teacher would say, 'since you've played a bit of football, I'll see you after school at Sydenham Oval.' It was like being given an order. So I turned up, and once they saw me on a football field their attitudes changed. That's who I was—a good athlete. I could've been graded.

As a kid, you don't appreciate the person standing in front of you trying to educate you. All it's like to a kid is a big grown-up saying, 'If ya don't do it, I'm gonna give you the strap.' In those days they gave you the cane.

I remember Charlie Carrol, Wayne Towney, and Danny Weldon—the four of us had a punch-on with some blokes from the football team. Although the others started it, we embarrassed the shit outa our sports teacher because we won the fight. We were playing a grade bigger than us—you know, taller—and we belted the shit outa them. When ya brought up in Redfern ya learn how to fight and scrap, take the good with the bad. It's like over in New York: if ya haven't been mugged by the time ya twelve, you're not a New Yorker. Same principle.

Anyway, our sports teacher got all the flak from the fight, so he took it out on us, and he gave us six on each hand. It's a big stick the cane—about four and a half feet long—and when he hit you on the knuckles, it stung like bloody hell. Our sports teacher was such a smart arse that when he went down with the cane, he'd bring it back up and catch the other side of your hand. So you got six on top and six underneath, as he was bringing the cane back up. Six down and six up, on each hand. Punishment was what I hated at school, but learning—I appreciated it. But I learned a whole lot by teaching myself. I taught myself that all this punishment I was getting was just for being myself, a Koori lad, and I made a vow that this treatment, meted out to me by people who really did not care, would not kill my spirit. I would fight against it forever if I had too!

I went to second form—that's year eight these days—but was forced to leave when I was fourteen because Mum needed the money. We were living at Portland Street, Waterloo, and I started working at Forthright's Ropes. The wage I ended up with was $24 a week. I had to stand in front of this machine, with about fifteen spools which the rope wound onto. When the rope was loaded onto the spool, I used to chop it, and tie it. It was very repetitive.

But I still had me mates. I was a workin man now. I was allowed to go out and I used to pay rent. Then I worked for a mob called Francis Chocolates. That was a production line too, where a lot of Kooris from Redfern worked. I wished I'd stayed in school, or had just one year away from the books. I wish now I'd been able to go right through school and on to university—the lot. If I ever have children of my own they are gonna go right through school. They're gonna have everything I never had. But the first thing they're gonna do is learn to paint, and I can teach them.

When Nobby grew into a teenager, about thirteen or fourteen, I'd see him and his big brother Billy getting dressed up and combing their hair.

'Where are you two boys goin?' I'd ask.

'We're goin chasin girls, Ma!'

'You'll go bald, you two, chasin gins against the wind!' And they'd bust out gigglin, goin out the door, cuddlin each other. They were real close my boys.

Darruk was the first boys' home I went to. I didn't last long there, I took off in the first three minutes, but I was caught again, and later did my sentence. The I got out and, with all the silly Koori mates in Redfern, it didn't take me long to get into trouble again. So I ended up in Mt Penang at Gosford like me true to form, there for a little till me old legs got the better of me and I took off again.

We had a big pig up there. I worked in the dairy, quite a few of us blokes got attached to this big pig. I won't mention his name because he became Sunday dinner! We saw him gettin into a truck, they said he was goin to the vet, and he came back alright, chopped up as dinner.

Although he'd spent time in the boys' homes for petty things, Nobby was not a hardened person. So he was knocked for a loop by the deaths of his brother and sister. They died within eight months of each other in 1969–1970. When his oldest sister, Pearl, was killed by a car, Nobby was brought from the boys' home in handcuffs for her funeral. And when Billy died, as a result of an epileptic seizure he took over the bath tub while trying to wash his jeans—in about eight inches of water he'd drowned—Nobby came in and lifted his dead brother's body up onto a bed. He covered Bill up with a blanket, then ran outa the house and never came back for days.

Nobby couldn't accept the fact of their deaths. It had a terrible effect on him. Besides, I was always saying to him, 'You're the eldest son now. You must be very responsible.' I sometimes think that my telling him that was very frightening to him, making him throw all caution to the winds, and get into trouble.

I was already in Darruk Boys' Home, out near Windsor, and I later found out that my brother David was in Darruk too, sentenced for a few months. Pretty soon I was back in the boob for punchin on with some bloke, and I was taken out to have a visit with Mum in the hall there, the gym it was. Terry, this mate of our family who had driven Mum and the kids out to visit us, had a big blue Ford. The visit was suddenly cancelled

*because a screw came running to take me back to the Pound.
I kissed Mum and the other kids goodbye and they put me
back into the boob, and I never found out until the next day
that this great mate of ours had kidnapped brother David out
of Darruk Boys' Home, put him in the boot of his car while
Mum was visitin me in the auditorium. He took off with him.
Everybody told me about it the next day. It was hilarious. Terry
did twelve months when they were caught and David ended
up back in Darruk Boys' Home again to finish his sentence.*

He was seventeen, had a girlfriend, but found her with
another bloke, got drunk to drown his sorrows, and got a
friend to drive him home to me in Green Valley. As the
young fella at the wheel was driving negligently, the police
chased them. There was a fourteen-year-old girl in the
back, who pulled a rifle out from under the seat and started
firing at the police. The kids stopped the car and took off
on foot, but the police caught them all. I went to the police
station at Bankstown to see Nobby, and I burst out cryin,
soon as I saw him, he had two black eyes and was holdin
on to the bars for support, he could hardly see out of his
eyes, and was cryin too. I demanded to know who'd done
this to him, the detectives and police laughed at me sayin,
'You watch Perry Mason too much, Mrs Langford, he fell
over when we were chasing him.' I screamed out, 'You
bastards, you're lyin!' And they were gonna charge me too
for offensive language! And I thought how could we ever
win in our own land with bastards like these police and
detectives?

On 21 June 1973, the *Telegraph* had this report: 'Two
teenagers charged with attempting to murder a police
constable appeared in separate courts yesterday . . .
Langford . . . was arrested at Rookwood Cemetery on
Tuesday after a high speed car chase . . .

How must he have felt?—a kid who went handcuffed

to his sister's funeral, who lifted his dead brother from the bath and laid him out, who drank to kill the pain, and who was arrested in a cemetery.

Another clipping from that time said: 'A 14-year-old girl was charged with shooting at a police constable with intent to murder after a running gun fight with a patrol car last night.'

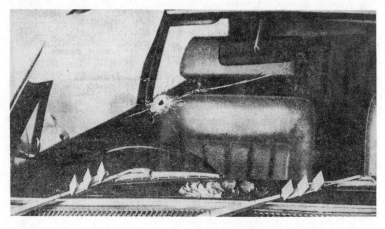

Reproduced with permission from the Sun, *20 June 1973*

What they forgot to mention was that this girl had gone Crown Witness to save her own skin, saying that Nobby had fired the gun. When it came time to go to court to answer the charges of 'attempted murder' and 'firing at police to escape lawful apprehension', I heard twelve police giving evidence, saying it was Nobby who fired the gun— though there were only two police in the car giving chase! I was thinking about that today, and the Royal Commission into Police Corruption in New South Wales, and I thought, How many other innocent people have been jailed because they never had money to pay corrupt police?

But back in 1973, the police had to have a conviction,

so they got the young girl to say Nobby was firing the gun. She and the other teenager, who was sixteen, went into juvenile custody. My son went to Long Bay Gaol at seventeen and a half years of age. That was the end of Nobby's childhood, and the end of my son's freedom. He did six years' jail for something he never did!

3

GUNGABULS

I was charged with attempted murder, and shooting with intent to avoid apprehension, and I would like to state for the record, for this book, that I did not shoot any gun. I was just in the car with the young girl and the young boy, and I was too drunk to probably even scratch myself, let alone pick up a gun and fire at a police officer.

It was very painful for Nobby to talk about these difficult times for this book. As well as wanting to forget the years he was incarcerated, he'd locked the memory of his brother's and sister's deaths away in a very secret part of his heart. He'd never allow any of us to speak their names.

He'd say, 'Don't get talkin about them, Mum. They're at peace now, resting. I can't stand you talking about them.' And he'd walk away.

But now I said, 'Listen, son. We must talk about our loved ones, and not just lock them away as though they never lived, cause their life had meaning and they really lived, you know. And we just can't lock them out forever. Besides, talking about them and how they were in the family with us keeps them close to us. I know it still pains you if anyone mentions their names. But if you want me to write your story with you, you've gotta sit down and talk to me and tell me things you couldn't tell me before.'

So when we started talking together I felt it was bringing us closer together. You see, I never really knew what it was like from his side of the prison wall, and he never knew what it was like from our side. Telling the story together made for better understanding.

I learnt about Nobby's feelings about death of loved family members, this incarceration, the whole corruption of the police and dicks—the so-called 'keepers of the laws' who turned out to be more corrupt than the people they were putting in jail.

He learned about my feelings of utter frustration of not being able to get any help for this son of mine who I know well enough to know he never fired at anyone! The torment of the rest of the family, my girls having bad dreams, nightmares about him being shot, not being able to visit and reassure him through lack of funds. It was endless sleepless nights having to impose on people to drive me and the kids to visit him, and because sometimes we couldn't go to visit him, the painful letters from him paying out on us, saying we didn't care, which tore us apart as a family. So helpless we were. In colonial courts in our own land!

We were glancing through the paper clippings I had kept all these years. Nobby and I had never looked at these clippings together. I kept all the clippings of all the reports written about the jail break in 1974. One of the prisoners in Nobby's wing bribed a screw for a key, and this fella went along and opened all the cells and they all ran.

'Do these clippings make you feel as upset as I do, Nob?' I asked. But then I said, 'Look at this picture of the ladder against the prison wall. I think it's bloody ingenious!'

'Yeah, it was made up of all the bed-heads tied together with torn up bits of sheets. And you can see from the picture of the cell block that the cells were definitely

opened from the outside,' Nob answered, and we had a
good chuckle about that. 'Bloody ingenious,' he echoed.

*But Mum, I remember the escape from Long Bay as a ter-
rifying experience. I was shit scared. We were over this building*

which was the old 4-Shop there at Long Bay Gaol. I remember leaning against this wall trying to hold this 25-foot ladder made out of bed ends and sheets all put together. We all decided to just get straight up and get over the wall. Then we held it back at the bottom about six foot so it would get a balance. It leaned against the top of the wall and as the first two went up the ladder—they got about eight foot off the ground—the bottom of the ladder broke. Then we picked the ladder up and moved it back and by this time an officer in the corner of the jail complex started shooting. The bullets were hitting parts of the ladder and the wall. We could hear them ricocheting. I was third up the ladder, and there was a friend of mine called Mouse who was behind me. You can imagine us tryin to get up this ladder as quick as possible. At the top of the ladder when I'd just put my leg over the top of the wall, and Mouse was coming up the ladder behind me, as I was getting balanced to just drop on the other side, his hand hit my foot, and I didn't land on the ground in too glamorous a pose—which is how I fractured my ankle.

But just through sheer panic and adrenaline I suppose, I got up and ran. I run straight for Anzac Parade, the main road that goes right past Long Bay Gaol. We run down towards the front of the old MTC. And then we jumped over the wall and ran straight across Anzac Parade. The four of us hit this cyclone fence at the same time, and it just kept going and landed under us on the ground, collapsed under our combined weight.

Then when I looked up to see where I was going, there was nobody else around me. So I run up behind this electrical box in this school yard, and then I saw this police car. As they were going around the power box I was going around the other side of it, so they couldn't see me. Lights were flashing and then they just took off in another direction. I hid till the car was out of sight and then I made my way towards the back of the school.

Once I was outside the school grounds, I did the 'backyard hop', which means you stay off the streets and go through the backyards and little lanes. And would you believe it?—in every fuckin yard I climbed into there was a dog. And in my panicked state, with the adrenaline pumping and the fear, I just started jumpin fences, and I just kept goin and goin and goin, and I didn't know what I was landin on—it could have been anything. Finally I got into this lane, and I was petrified that the cops would come around the corner, so I just kept to the shadows, hid behind cars until I was safely out of the sounds of the sirens.

Of all the escapees, the last one to be caught was my so-called 'dangerous criminal' son. But Nobby wasn't half as dangerous as the cops who came after him.

At the time of the break-out from the Bay, my eldest daughter Dianne was living in Clara Street, Erskineville. My other son, David, lived there with her. David had the same facial features as Nobby, only he was dark skinned and short like me. A few days after this break-out happened, David went out to try and draw the cops off his brother's tracks. He had a mate with a ute truck, and he took it out zig-zaggin all over the road and because David looked like Nobby, the police raided Dianne's house one night with guns, screaming out, 'We got him! We got Langford!'

Dianne told me it scared the bloody hell out of her, waking with a start, her bed surrounded by coppers, with guns pointed at her head. Little did Dianne know that David had run upstairs and hidden under her bed while she was asleep. You should have seen the looks on the cops' faces when they pulled David out and found he wasn't Nobby. They took David down to the CIB headquarters and gave him a good kickin. They took Dianne too in her nightclothes. Didn't even give her a chance to change. Afterwards, there was nothing we could do but nurse David's bruises. We know that the Redfern cops are the pits; ask any Koori who lives there.

*Reproduced with permission from
the* Daily Telegraph, *6 August 1974*

*Anyway, my freedom. Near the end of the very short ten days
I was out, I was over in Lilyfield near Leichhardt when the
police surrounded the house that I was in. I escaped in a yellow
Lotus Europa, police in hot pursuit. I got out of the car after
the police car rammed me, and I run through some backyards
and hid under this car. But a few hours later I was appre-
hended. They had so many police there, you'd think the Queen
of England was over here for a holiday.*

*They took me to the CIB in Central and proceeded to kick
the shit outa me. They charged me with car stealing and escape
from lawful custody. I was remanded in custody, obviously, and
taken straight from the police cells to Parramatta Circle. It was
run on the same lines as Alcatraz in America. The Circle in*

31

those days in Parramatta was, besides Grafton, probably the most high security intractable jail in Australia. Anyway, I was put there with the rest of my cronies, who had already been arrested prior, and we all fronted court on the same day two weeks later.

At the same time as we were going to court at Central, the Bathurst jail riots boys were all going too. They were talking to us and asking, 'How'd youse do it?'—just normal jail talk. This and that. Then it was time for us all to go to court, the five of us that escaped from the Bay. And they just adjourned it for reports or whatever, this and that. But as I was being taken out of the court room, the two police officers who were goose-stepping me out of the court just threw me through a bloody door. It had a big glass partition at the top. They threw me bodily through it. The door was in splinters and glass was everywhere. I was all cut up. But THEY charged ME with assaulting police!

It was Mr Murray Farquar, CSM, who remanded Nobby to Central Court on 22 August. I got to thinkin about that name, Farquar, the magistrate. He was later jailed for perverting the course of justice, but at that time he was sitting in judgement of my son! Some great law-keepers they have in this country, aye? He ended up in Berrima Jail makin clocks and he died in December 1993.

Nobby was sentenced to a further two and a half years with no parole period—a straight two and a half years.

Anyway, I was thrown to the system after getting let out of the Circle after twelve months, and I was put down into a boys' jail at Goulburn. It was the coldest cunt of a place I've ever been in my life. Anyway I didn't last long down there—three months to be exact.

Because it was a boys' jail, three of my other mates who went over the wall with me at Long Bay were also sent down there, and we wanted to get out of Goulburn because it was so bloody cold. I was only nineteen at the time, and we got what's called 'shanghaied' by the Mod Squad—which means being transferred, without warning, to another jail. The Mod Squad, who moved inmates from jail to jail, had batons and Christ knows what else, and tear gas. So we went with them up to Long Bay for a couple of days. Shortly after that, this is 1975, we ended up at Maitland Jail.

It was just after the Maitland riots, which followed the Bathurst riots in a chain reaction, and we were all intractables shanghaied from another jail.

The Bathurst jail riots were over poor conditions because Michael Yabsley, the then Minister for Corrective Services—also a descendant of the first squatters who dispossessed my people of their land in Bundjalung country—had thrown the prison system into turmoil by de-humanising prisoners: by confiscating their wedding rings. They were allowed only a few family photos, I think three only, and a certain amount of tapes for their cassettes, no education, no art supplies, also shocking food. That's why they rioted. And this dehumanising system caused a chain reaction of rioting throughout the NSW prisons, Bathurst, Maitland, Goulburn, and Long Bay.

We were all locked up for a few days. The Crown, or the Governor, or whoever was in power up there got us all out and decided to make us—the sixteen blokes that got shanghaied from Goulburn—the sweepers of the jail. That meant you gave out the toothpaste, toilet paper, tea and whatever. So us boys became the sweepers of the jail.

When we got out of the van at Maitland Jail, we were all handcuffed together two at a time. And we had to run through a gauntlet to get to B-Wing in the jail. It was made up of two rows of officers, one row on either side of us. I was handcuffed to a really small mate of mine, who was about eight stone wringing wet, and when the batons hit him on the head I picked him up because I couldn't drag him along the ground. I had to pick him up to get inside B-Wing, out of the line of this gauntlet.

As I picked up the little bloke, a baton hit me on my left thumb. I know the name of the officer that hit me and he did lay the boot in after a while when I went down. Anyway, we eventually got to B-Wing. After a time I was taken to the clinic with my thumb the way it was, and then they took me to Maitland Hospital where the doctor said my thumb had to be rebroken. So I went to the jail and they gave me painkillers for a few more days, and bandaged me up. Then I was taken to Long Bay Gaol where I was put in to Prince Henry Hospital and they did reconstruction on my left thumb. It's now had two lots of reconstructive surgery on it, but it's still never been the same.

I was brought back from the hospital to Long Bay to await the escort back to Maitland. Anyway, there was a little Koori fella there. He used to sort of faint every time he walked outside the wing in the morning for musters, and he always looked really pale and sickly. We found out that his cell mate was stealing all of his food. This was why the little bloke was so weak all the time. While my mates were all arguing who was going to chop into this bloke, I took the initiative and nearly killed him in the yard. The officers came and dragged us apart. I had a lot of blood on me but none of it was me own. It was just the sheer hatred of somebody stealing food out of a little blackfella's mouth, denying him his food. It was bad enough that he was in jail. You don't steal food off another inmate regardless of what colour you are. But for protecting the little Koori fella, I was charged with assaulting a fellow prisoner. I got 24 hours in the cells.

Over the next five years I was in custody, I had three other charges for misconduct. On 3 September 1976, I was charged

34

with assault of a prisoner officer—five days in the cells. That was unavoidable: I was working in the Parramatta laundry, and every Monday we had to take up barrows full of sheets that were taken out of the wings and we had to make sure there was nothing inside the bundle. This officer went over them with a metal detector. One bundle kept setting the thing off for no reason. Anyway, the fourth time I undid this same bundle of sheets there was again nothing in there. I counted each sheet back in there but his metal detector kept going off. I said, 'Fuck it, I'm not doing this again.' The officer manhandled me, grabbed me and pushed me into the pile of sheets, so I elbowed him in the guts. I got five days in the cells for that.

Although Nobby had some hard times in Parramatta, he asked to be transferred there from Maitland after all his cell property was destroyed.

The Movements Officer came around to Maitland. His name was Paul Jenner. He looked at me and said, 'Nobby, you're in trouble again.'

I said, 'I'd like to know who smashed all me cell property.' Because, when we arrived at Maitland, all we had was smashed, so we just had the clothes we were wearing and a toothbrush and toothpaste. My cellmate and I at Goulburn had $200 dollars worth of food that we'd accumulated over a couple of weeks, but when we got our property back, after the move to Maitland Jail, every jar was smashed. There was honey all through our letters. You couldn't keep them. You just had to throw em away.

But anyway, Jenner said, 'What am I gonna do to keep you out of trouble?'

'You send me to Parramatta Jail to finish my sentence,' I replied, 'And you'll never hear from me ever again.'

'You've gotta give me your word on that.'

I said, 'You've got it.'

'OK,' he said, and three days later I was back at Parramatta Jail—the best jail in the state in those days.

One thing I liked about jail, Mum, was the football. The Parramatta Pirates we were called and we were an awesome team. There was me, Allan and Patrick (me adopted brothers), and Franky Vincent, little Freddy Owens, Johny Pride, and Kev Holland, our captain coach. We threw out a challenge to all the big A-grade footballers. We played HMAS Hobart—defeated em 48–nil, and Phoenix 33–3. We drew with Liverpool 18–all.

The Pirates were written up in the *Rugby League Week*. It said their playing field in Parramatta Jail was once a rock quarry. The idea to convert it into a playing field was thought up by seven prisoners who were keen Rugby League men. They put the idea to the head warden and he agreed to allow the prisoners to commence work on the project. Today the field is one of the best looked after grounds in Australia. The *Rugby League Week* article mentions:

. . . class performance by Peter Pool who toils for 80 minutes every game, and Paul Blacklock, who plays better football than his brother Ray [an A-grade player from Penrith]. There's not much of little Freddie Owens size-wise, but he more than makes up for it in heart. Not forgetting the honest toilers, Kevin Kemp, Frank Vincent, and hard-tackling Nobby Langford.

When Nobby was first incarcerated I vowed I wouldn't go into jails any more to visit, not only because some were too far away, but because it distressed me so much. I'd always hype myself up and always took some family member along to keep me company, though I'd mostly always come away cryin anyway, but I never let Nobby see my tears. I always went in 'laughin like a clown'.

But I went to visit Nobby on his 21st birthday—me and his old tribal uncle, James Golden. I had a guitar that I'd bought for him as a present. The governor said he could have it. Nobby was in Prince Henry Hospital at the time with a broken thumb from playin that damned football. At the hospital we were searched before entering. He was propped up in bed with a guard who was looking after some other prisoners too. When I gave him a cuddle, saying, 'I got ya guitar for you son,' he whispered in my ear: 'Give me that ring please, Mum, for a keepsake.'

'How?' I asked. 'They'll search ya and you'll get into more trouble.'

'No I won't. Not here,' he said. 'Take it off and push it down here,' he said, pointing to his bandaged hand.

I did his bidding, glancing around to see if anyone was watching. I'd probably end up in jail with my son too if they caught us! But they didn't and that ring did two years' jail with him, just keeping him company. I chuckled to myself, rememberin.

When we were chuckling I was thinkin there was also some very painful things that happened in jails.

You have to be bloody well strong in jail; if they think you're a pansy you'll cop it. You have to be on your guard all the time. I've seen men raped, bashed, 'stikem'—stuck with a knife. You learn to keep ya bloody mouth shut if you know what's good for you. They don't suffer 'stoolies' in prison—that's what they call the ones that give people up to the police. 'Dogs'— nobody will have anything to do with them; they're treated with contempt by the big boys. And child-bashers and women-bashers, they get their just desserts in there. That's where they separate the men from the boys, Mum. They call the child-

molesters 'rock spiders'. They have to be segregated from the rest or else they'll get belted.

In jail—and being a person who knows quite a bit about it—I can say that you've got different cliques. You've got the Aborigines, the Greeks, the Italians, and now you've got the Vietnamese. The Lebanese too—all different nationalities. All being put into jail for one thing and another. Obviously you've got some people or officers who don't like Aborigines, or they don't like Greeks, or Italians or Christ knows what. You've gotta stick very close with your clique. And if you have a drama with, say, the Lebanese or something, and your little clique doesn't help you, you're gone.

Once you go to jail with people who've known you all your life, you automatically get put into their clique. Then ya get white people sayin, 'Look at that bunch of black bastards with that white fellow over there.' But then the shoe can be put on the other foot: I know a lot of really nasty Kooris. But I also know a lot of nasty, vindictive white people. I think the whites outweigh the black people, because so many white people are really racist towards any indigenous people, or any black people. They also give the Vietnamese heaps, give the Chinese heaps— any nationality other than white Australians. Lots of white Australians think they're God!

Nobby told me about one of his friends that he grew up with in Redfern. I'll call him Jack so his relatives won't be offended if they read this. Like so many of our people, Jack was illiterate; like so many of our people, he'd had religion rammed down his throat at an early age. Because he had psychological problems, like a lot of our mob, he was kept in a special wing. There the religious instructor—I don't know if he was a pastor, or minister, or priest—used to visit Jack and read him parts of the Bible. He'd tell him, 'If thine eye offends thee, pluck it out!' One day Jack was doing some art, and these words were going around and around in his head. He up with his paint brush and, placing the pointed end on his eye, he hit it hard with his other hand. It killed him instantly, piercing his brain. He became another statistic, another Aboriginal death in custody.

After telling me about this, Nobby said, 'Mum, I can't tell you any more. It's too painful. He was my friend. I'd known him since we was teenagers.' It seemed there was no end to the sorrow, cruelty, and death. But enough! Enough! I did not want to hear any more myself, cause it made me weep, just hearing this sadness.

But there was also a lot of sadness for us, outside the prison walls. Each time Nob was jailed the whole family went with him. I said to Nob, 'You've never done jail by yourself, son, cause every time you went to jail, we the family went with you. It was the most traumatic time for our family. When you ran, we ran too. When you were bashed, we felt it too! You have always been covered by our family's love.'

That's the only thing that kept me sane.

When Nobby was first jailed, and on the run after the break-out, his sister Ellen would run each morning up to the shop to get the early papers, then they'd all be scanning them for news of their brother. They would also listen to the radio all gathered around, listening intently for any information about him, the sad, lost, looks on their faces showing their anguish about Nobby. 'Mum, the police might shoot him,' Pauline said, burstin into tears, with Aileen comforting her. 'Don't say that, Pauline, he's a survivor, he's gotta be,' I echoed.

Jeffery, the youngest brother who played football like big brother for Green Valley and Sadlier, he'd be having nightmares, wakin up singing out, 'Nobby, Nobby.' I had to sit with him and soothe him until he went off to sleep again with his football in his arms.

4

HOME COMMIN

When Nob finished his prison sentence in December 1978, he was 23 years old. After being locked away for almost six years, everything was so strange to him. I never understood how much of an impact prison had on people, not only my son. Nobby would lock himself away in the bedroom by himself. I was rushing around trying to make him feel welcome by cookin up his favourite foods—spaghetti, steak with garlic and onion gravy. But he said to me, 'Mum, don't fuss. Leave me to myself. I'll eat afterwards.' I was so hurt, thinkin he don't want the family around him.

But it wasn't that, he explained later. It was the shock, after years of being locked away, of being hit head-on with all the noise and bustle of the outside world. Even the crying of the two babies I was lookin after, my grandchildren Roberta and Ronny-boy, stressed Nob so much he'd have to go out walkin to get away from the sound. It freaked him out so much. He wanted to go to Eveleigh Street to visit his sister Dianne, but he was afraid of catching the train. He went eventually with his sister Aileen for company.

The cops never left him alone. They were always checkin up on him. The cops never let anyone out of their sight who had been charged with offences against them. He could be 'verballed' again for anything—verballing means when police concoct a story about you, or say you confessed to a crime. They lay charges against you, and other police verify their story. These days, verballing can't happen because all statements made to police are recorded. But back in 1978, Nobby was at the mercy of the police.

He got so run down he got hepatitis. He was real sick, bedridden. I told the story in *Don't Take Your Love to Town* about how the Liverpool police came to our place at Green Valley and hassled him. They knocked on the door, and when I opened it they pushed right past me. They didn't hear me at first when I told them Nobby was sick. They just bowled right into the room. I said, 'I hope you've all had your shots; he's got contagious hepatitis.' You should have seen those gungies fly outa the room, asking where the nearest doctor's surgery was. Nob and I fell about laughing.

After Nobby came out and moved to Camperdown from Green Valley, we'd all meet up at the Clifton Hotel in Redfern. I remember him and David's blue there, when Nobby smashed the windows of David's car because their old girlfriends used to play brother off against brother: by carryin yarns, back and forth, which I thought was a low act. Anyway, when the cops came round the corner, David said, 'Piss off Nobby, here comes the Gungie.' But Nobby just stood there sayin, 'I'm not goin, Bra. If they take you, they can take me too!' I had to hold my hand over my mouth so they couldn't hear me gigglin, because it didn't take my boys long to pull together and forget their blue, when the odds were stacked against them.

Then Nobby, who was pretty pissed, sauntered off up the hill after the police drove off, yelling out, 'I don't want any more to do with my family.'

A week later, he walked into David's place in Redfern

and put $200 into his hands for the smashed car windows and they were huggin and forgivin each other, my two sons makin amends.

During the week, Nobby worked hard at a picture framing place called Geometrics, in Ultimo. He worked there for two and a half years and was a very trusted employee. He had a position of responsibility as he had to open the factory for early starts.

I had to give up the home in Green Valley because all the kids had moved on with their lives, so I didn't need a big four-bedroom home for just me, Jeffery, my youngest, and Aileen, my sixth child. Besides, it was lonely in the valley after all the mob was gone. So I moved, with Jeff and Aileen, into a place in Charles Street, Erskineville.

Nobby used to do some deliveries in that area, and one day he pulled into our driveway, and what a shock I got! There was his pet cat, a white tomcat, sitting perched on his shoulder while he was driving the van. I thought to myself, 'What next?' The cat he'd named Warlock had a small silver chain around its neck, and when Nobby was walking to the shop or payin his rent, the cat trotted along beside him like a dog. He loved that cat. I remember when Warlock got into a fight with some other tomcats and they nearly ripped his eye out, Nobby had him at the vet's getting microsurgery. He was in such a state worrying about his pet that he was down at the Clifton Hotel drowning his sorrows in beer, crying over that damned cat.

With Jeff and Aileen, I moved from Erskineville to Zetland, and then to Pritchard Street, Marrickville. I set it up with the landlord for Nobby and one of my adopted sons, Patrick, to rent the house next door to me. Nob had changed jobs, and worked at L.N.C. Industrial Sheetmetal Workers. He got Patrick a start there too. But that was only for about nine months. When he was outa work, Nobby got real depressed.

I remember he had an argument with his latest

girlfriend, and he was even rowing with me, and he locked himself away next door with some grog and took some sleeping pills. Me and my daughter Ellen got worried because we didn't see him for hours, so Ellen jumped the back fence. After, we nearly knocked the door down tryin to get in, and we found him unconscious—he'd overdosed. We called an ambulance and took him to Marrickville Hospital where they pumped his stomach out. Me and Ellen were frantic. It freaked us right out!

Soon as he was conscious he ran out of the hospital with only his trousers on, no shirt or shoes, running wild-eyed like a frightened animal.

Then someone told him there was work to be done in the fruit areas of South Australia, so he loaded up his trusty old Valiant, and left for South Australia, tellin me he'd keep in touch. A month went by. No word. Then I woke up one morning to a loud knocking on the door, to find him standing in the doorway in a tracksuit with his duffle bag in his hand. He looked terrible.

It was wintertime and he was freezing because he didn't have a jacket or jumper on, besides, he was physically exhausted.

'What's happened, son?' I asked.

'Mum, I've just hitched all the way from South Australia. Even had to sell the car to put a feed in my mouth. It was bloody terrible! No work there and the cops on ya soon as ya go into the townships.'

What a rough time my son'd had. To top it all off, I had to tell him that his beloved dog, Napoleon, had been killed by a truck while he was away.

Anyway, he registered up for the dole, and moved in next door again with Patrick. These little places in Pritchard Street only had two small bedrooms, but we mucked in and made them liveable. But Nobby couldn't seem to kick on with a job, and he got really depressed again. So

I said to him one day, after he'd been job huntin, 'Look, son, you don't have to walk for miles and miles. Just go around close to here. There's lots of factories.' So away he went, and pretty soon I heard him coming back down the lane. He was whistling, and I knew he'd found a job. When he walked in the door, he had the biggest grin on his face.

'I got a start at Datamail, Mum, just down around the corner!'

'Good on ya, son. I knew you'd find a job.'

While he was at Datamail he met Anna, at the place where he used to buy his lunch. The old love bug bit him again. She was Portuguese, only a little thing, and she had two children.

When Patrick got married in June 1984, Nobby moved to Clara Street, Erskineville with Anna. Her two children loved him like he was their real dad. Nobby got stuck into his work. He won $4000 in a scratch lottery ticket and bought himself a Toyota ute so he could become a courier. Phillip White, his neighbour, had told him 'Ya can make good bloody money doin that, mate.' And pretty soon, Nobby *was* earning good money and, bein a workaholic, he was doin runs all over the place.

On 29 November 1984, my son David, the 28-year-old father of two children, died from a drug overdose. Nobby was inconsolable; they were so close these two sons of mine. We called them 'the long and short of it' because Nobby was 6 foot 2 inches and Dave was 5 foot 5 inches tall.

At David's funeral, Nobby was so distressed. In his grief he screamed out after the funeral service, 'Not him! Not him! Why couldn't God take me? I'm the criminal. Not him!' I had to lead him away from David's casket, so they could put it in the hearse.

Anna said he was drinking heavily and she was worried about him. Several times she told me she couldn't find him after these drinking bouts. One time she followed him and found him sleeping on David's and Bill's grave out at Botany Cemetery.

I tried to talk to him about the drinking, but it was just like pouring water on a duck's bloody back. After a while he seemed to settle down, but it was a terrible time in our family's life.

At that time, Anna was workin too, so Nobby applied for a home loan, and surprised himself by gettin it. Fifty-eight thousand dollars he borrowed, and they don't give these home loans to bums, aye.

Nobby and Anna purchased one of those long homes in Plumpton in the west of Sydney. This new home wasn't landscaped, so Nobby spent hours working in the garden of a weekend. He built a barbecue, and it all looked beautiful. Matter of fact, it was the first place in the street to be landscaped. It really was a credit to him, and they were steadily paying it off when, with the agony of his brother's death still haunting him, he started to fall to pieces.

There was also trouble between him and Anna. Anna, not knowing how to cope if Nobby wasn't home from work on time, would be ringing me and other members of the family up, checkin on him all the time. Lots of times he came to see me and Jeff, and he told me, 'I've got away from jail, where I was bein watched all the time, but now in my own home I'm still being watched—by Anna, 24 hours a day!' When they had a blue over his drinkin, she'd take the kids and go to her sister's place.

There were also great financial stresses, what with paying of the house and everything. Nob took to driving the Toyota half-pissed. He smashed into the back of another car in his courier van.

On 13 November 1985, Nobby was convicted of 'Driving whilst disqualified', 'Failure to stop', and 'Negligent driving'. He was fined $800, $300 and $100 respectively, and given eight months to pay. He was also disqualified from driving for six months.

New South Wales Government
Department of Corrective Services

PRE-SENTENCE REPORT
NOBBY LANGFORD
D.O.B. 21/5/55

Redfern Local Court: 13/11/85

Mr Langford is a 30 year old employed man of Aboriginal descent who resides with his de facto wife and her children . . .

OFFENCE

Mr Langford admits to the offences for which he is charged. He states that he panicked following the collision and impulsively left the scene . . .

ASSESSMENT

Mr Langford is a man who has, in the last two and a half years, made enormous gains in his personal life and endeavoured to lead a socially acceptable lifestyle. The offender has presented a very different picture from the man who from 1969 to 1982 spent much of his time involved in a criminal lifestyle . . .

L.J. Loutides,
Probation and Parole Officer,
Newtown District Office.

13 November, 1985.

Nobby couldn't work as a courier after this. But he found

another job as storeman-packer at AWA in Ashfield. He had to get up around 4am to catch a train from Rooty Hill station, and he wouldn't get home till about six or seven o'clock each night. Boy, what a let down from bein a courier!

So the stresses on Nob were all piling up. He was drinkin to keep from worryin about the fines and the house repayments and his troubles with Anna, and David's death. The final straw was when he found out it was hard drugs that had killed David. Nobby just fell to pieces. I never showed Nobby the coroner's report, because I knew it would distress him more, but someone hit David up with the hard drugs that killed him. And besides, I knew I couldn't hide this from him forever, so I had to tell Nobby the truth. He had had enough! He wanted to die, and be with David and Bill, the brothers he loved.

Nobby lay down in the middle of the road, wanting a bloke in a Mack truck to run over him. When the truck driver wouldn't do this, Nobby started ripping off the rear vision mirror, and the windscreen wipers of the truck. For this Nobby was charged with malicious injury. This was 16 April 1986.

When the police were called, they soon had him down with his face pressed into the bitumen of the road, with their feet holding him down on the gravel. He was charged with resisting arrest. A girl that had grown up with Nob in Redfern told me about how the police treated him. She had heard the commotion, come out the front of her house, and when she saw it was Nobby, she started yelling at the police, 'Let him up! He's not an animal!' They told her to shut up, or they'd pinch her too. Nobby was very drunk and was struggling to get up. For that he was charged with assaulting the police.

All this was a cry for help from Nobby. But instead of taking him to a psychiatric centre for counselling, they took him back to the police cells and bashed him. He came out looking, in his own words, like the elephant man.

Nobby was seeing a Dr Kordik at Polyclinic Mt Druitt to sort himself out. He was a psychiatrist. When a Koori person has a breakdown, it's very easy for people to blame that person alone, because they do not understand that that person's breakdown is part of a bigger historical picture. They never look at the dispossession, the having to conform to other people's laws, rules, and standards. Koori people have never been able to be themselves. We were forced to assimilate, and never had a choice. My son is fair, and looks like a whiteman, but he says, 'I'm a black man wrapped up in a white skin!' And all the trauma he's had to cope with throughout his life has been bound up with this identity crisis that goes right back to when he was very young. He never knew who he really was.

My son's story is not only his story but the story of many others. Speaking of her own family's experience, Aboriginal Magistrate Pat O'Shane wrote that:

> I recognised all the things that happened to me through my grandparents, and their parents; their brothers and sisters; through my mother and her siblings; through my cousins and my siblings, the things that happened to thousands of other Aboriginal families, and I marvelled, THAT WE ALL WEREN'T STARK RAVING MAD![1]

Nobby wasn't going mad, but he *was* having a nervous breakdown. Anna took off to her sister's again, and me and Jeffery got a phone call. Their union didn't last long because she'd never been involved with anyone who'd been in jail before, but he did love her and the children she had, treated them as his own.

Nobby sounded so dejected. He wanted us to come and get him. When me and Jeffery arrived at his place, he was like a lost soul. He had a little bag packed and he was cuddlin his dog, Pippa. He was so sad and distressed. So hurt. I could see that he was falling apart. I can see him now, sitting in the back seat of Jeffery's car, holding on to his dog.

We took him to my place in Henderson Road, and I rang up a psychiatric centre called the Langton Clinic. I made an appointment for Nobby to see a psychiatrist the next day. We bedded him down, and he made his dog lie down at his feet before he nodded off to sleep. I was real worried about him. He was in bad shape.

Nobby went to keep the appointment next day, and he came back sayin he was goin to Brisbane to my sister Rita's, as he needed to sort himself out. Some friend who owed Nobby a favour from jail had given him a car and a few hundred dollars. We didn't know at the time that he'd given Nobby a gun too. Some great friend *he* was! If we'd known about the gun, we would've taken it off him. So away to Brisbane he went. We waved him off, Jeffery and me. I was terrified of letting Nobby go, he'd be breaking parole, not fronting up at court, and most of all I worried about his state of mind over the loss of his brother David, as well as Bill and Pearl.

Learning of the circumstances of my brother David's death— that he died from a drug overdose—actually shattered me. I think I was the one who suffered the most trauma after his death for reasons I'd like to hold to myself. After seeing a psychiatrist, trying to sort myself in relation to my brother's death, I needed to get out of Sydney and take a rest. I decided to visit my auntie in Queensland to get away from all my problems and my feelings of grief about David's death. I went up north but didn't stay long, and I was all the time thinking about the fact that my brother had died from an OD on heroin. I couldn't believe it.

And then because I had only one brake light, the police chased me. A police officer started following me in a car, and as I was unlicensed I just took off. I had a .38 handgun in the car and on the spur of the moment I stopped the car and got out. I wanted to stop the car from chasing me. I stopped my car and the police car stopped about 50 feet behind me. I stepped out of the car, aimed at the police car and shot two bullets into the radiator. Then I took off, abandoned the car, and was later arrested in the bush.

PROBATION AND PAROLE SERVICE
PAROLE REPORT
NOBBY LANGFORD

Date of Birth: 21st May, 1955

On the 10th of August, 1986, Mr. Langford was arrested in Armidale and charged with resisting arrest, shooting at police, and possession of an unlicensed pistol. Mr. Langford was remanded in custody on this matter to Maitland Gaol. Mr. Langford has recently been transferred to Parklea Prison in Sydney, allowing interview by this officer. Mr. Langford then indicated that there were other outstanding charges of 'Assault' and 'Resist Arrest' relating to a domestic incident. On the 19th December, 1986, Mr. Langford will be applying for bail at the District Court.

Mr. Langford has made contact with the psychiatrist he has at Mt. Druitt and requested a consultation. The doctor does not attend people in prison but has indicated that he would see Mr. Langford when he is released on bail. Should Mr. Langford obtain bail, he considers his first priority is psychiatric treatment and his second, employment, as he is several house payments behind and gravely concerned about losing his house . . .

The serious nature of the charges Mr. Langford is facing and his breach of conditions in leaving the State as notified by the parolee in his recent interview in gaol is regrettable because of the satisfactory response he had been making in 1984 and 1985.

L.J. Loutides,
Probation and Parole Officer,
NEWTOWN DISTRICT OFFICE.

19th December, 1986.

PROBATION AND PAROLE SERVICE
NOBBY LANGFORD

Langford's prime offence for which he is on parole goes back to the 20th June, 1973 when he was sentenced to twelve and a half years [Nobby had to serve six years of a ten-year sentence before parole, then the two years added on for break-out made it twelve years] for maliciously shooting to prevent apprehension, and breaking, entering and stealing. The charges against him of 13 April, 1986, and 10 August 1986, appear to be of a similar nature. I understand from Ms Loutides that he has acknowledged that he took the pistol with him to Queensland ostensibly for his protection and he hoped to avoid what he alleges was police harassment in Sydney. While there may be some logic from his point of view, the fact is that he has acknowledged a serious criminal offence to avoid apprehension while on parole, his possession of the pistol, and that he actually fired the pistol to avoid apprehension. He also drove his vehicle while disqualified. While there was improvement in his behaviour in 1984 and 1985, little confidence could be had for his behaviour in 1986. I recommend revocation.

Nigel Stoneman,
Officer-in-Charge,
NEWTOWN DISTRICT OFFICE.

22nd December, 1986.

CONFIDENTIAL

Psychological Report
8 July, 1987

Re: *Nobby Langford*

I saw Langford at the Parklea Prison on 24 June, 1987. He is 32 years of age and he is charged with discharging a firearm in an attempt to avoid lawful apprehension and some related offences . . .

Langford said that five days before these offences occurred his mother had told him the circumstances of his brother's death some eighteen months previously. He said she had told him that his brother had died of an overdose of heroin. Langford said, 'When she told me I got really upset. I was shattered . . . I wasn't thinking right . . . . I've been the one who has been in trouble and he had really got up and given it a go and there he was dead. She showed me the autopsy report . . . This is the third [member of my] family I have lost!'

Langford said that he had been going through a hard time prior to this. He said he had been stood off from work at AWA, [and] . . . could not get another job . . . He said '*I didn't know how we were going to manage. I tried everywhere for work out in the area, and I couldn't find anything. Anna had two kids to look after . . . [and] hasn't been working either because of the kids. I was fearful I was going to lose my house.*'

Langford went on to describe how he had driven to Brisbane and while he was driving up he had felt quiet and happy . . . but when he got to Brisbane he felt very restless. He said, '*I couldn't sit down for five minutes. I wasn't sleeping and I wasn't eating much. Then I got this phone call and someone said Anna was missing. I said to my aunt I was going home. My aunt tried to stop me going home. I headed back to Sydney. I pulled over on Saturday night somewhere near Armidale and I went to sleep. I'd just woken*

up and got going when this highway patrol came up behind me. I
pulled over. I never had a proper licence. I didn't trust myself to
pass the test. I handed them my forklift driver's licence. I just went
completely over the top and took off. About three kms down the road
I was pulled over. I was loading the gun. I jumped out and fired
two shots at the radiator of their car. There was no intention of
shooting them—I just wanted to be by myself.' [Nobby was frightened to ever front for a licence in his own name because of his
police records, so he did the next best thing, he got an illegal
one. He paid $300 for it, and I laughed when he showed me.
In those days you could get a bodgie licence supplied by crook
Department of Motor Transport people, these licences had the
names and birthdays of deceased people: his was Josep Kalanji.
That's why I was laughin. I said to him, 'You don't look like a
"Josep Kalanji" to me. That's a "wog" new Australian name.
You're flat out trying to be known as a Koori.' And he said,
'Shut the fuck up, Mum. I've gotta work you know.']

Langford said that he cannot really explain why he behaves
the way he does at times. He said that when something goes
wrong in his life he gets very upset. He said he just seems to
get hyped up and doesn't know what he is doing . . . He said
that when things are going well with him he will not drink at
all but if he gets upset he is likely to drink heavily. He said that
after his brother died he was drinking heavily and he admitted
himself to the Langton Clinic because he realised he was drinking too much . . .

Langford is the sort of man who presents society with a real
dilemma. In lots of ways he is quite a likeable man and given a
reasonable chance he is hard working and industrious and
devoted to his family. One cannot but feel that he has experienced hardship in his life and that looked at from a sociological
point of view he has not had much of a chance to go straight.
Just when he seems to be getting in the clear with a home and
family and a job he loses the job and he is back to square one
again and he is under a great deal of emotional pressure. From

the psychiatric point of view he has got a hysterical personality disorder. He behaves histrionically and impulsively in response to emotional stresses in his life. This is characterised by his histrionic action of throwing himself in front of a truck in April of 1986, his behaviour at his brother's funeral and now his histrionic distress over learning about the nature of his brother's death. He is, in a sense, an emotionally unstable man and his behaviour with respect to these charges reflects all of that emotional instability . . . He seems to have trouble keeping himself out of trouble because of his impulsiveness . . . He also seems to lack foresight. He did not seem to understand that once he had a clean record he should have been able to get himself a legitimate licence . . .

There are some indications that at least over the last few years Langford has been making an effort to curb his impulsiveness and stay out of trouble. There seems to be no way that he is going to avoid a custodial sentence . . . but at least the plea might be made that the sentence is not so savage as to destroy what hope there might be for the process of rehabilitation of this man to be continued. Hopefully, while he is in gaol he will get some sympathetic counselling and the capacity he has displayed to apply himself to work will be capitalised upon as far as is possible in the prison system and he will be prepared for employment when he comes out.

Yours faithfully,
Dr William Barclay

IN THE DISTRICT COURT
OF NEW SOUTH WALES
CRIMINAL JURISDICTION
BEFORE HIS HONOUR JUDGE MOSS

MONDAY 27 July 1987

REGINA v Nobby LANGFORD

CHARGE: (1)   For that he on 10 August 1986 near Uralla, in the State of New South Wales did maliciously discharge loaded arms with intent to prevent lawful apprehension.

PLEA: Guilty

CHARGE: (2)   For that he on 10 August 1986 near Uralla, in the State of New South Wales did use a pistol not being an antique pistol, to wit, a .38 calibre revolver, he not being the holder of a pistol licence in respect of such pistol.

PLEA: Guilty

MR CHEGWIDDEN appeared for the Crown.
MR DOWD appeared for the prisoner.

PRISONER
Sworn to answer:
CROSS EXAMINATION

MR CHEGWIDDEN: Q. The police asked you about the motor vehicle and you said: *'I was supposed to front court on the 5th and I did not. I got the car off a bloke I knew in gaol, I knew years ago. He owed me a few favours so he got me the car and the gun and he*

55

gave me 500 bucks and a bodgy label. He told me to ring back in a week.'

A. Yes.

Q. Then shortly afterwards the police asked you the circumstances in relation to the gun and you replied, *'It was given to me by the guy that gave me the car and he just said "Look after yourself"'*?

A. Yes.

Q. Why did you need a gun to look after yourself?

A. Somebody could have hijacked me on the highway. Anything could have happened and in my mind I did not know what I was doing.

Q. I take it you did not have the gun expecting the police would be after you in relation to your non-appearance in court?

A. No.

Q. You were not expecting a shoot out with the police?

A. No.

Q. Just in case you got hijacked you got a gun, is that right?

A. You need to protect yourself these days.

Q. You considered it necessary to have a gun in order to protect yourself in this community, do you? (objected to)

IN THE DISTRICT COURT
OF NEW SOUTH WALES
CRIMINAL JURISDICTION
BEFORE HIS HONOUR JUDGE MOSS

MONDAY 27 July 1987

REGINA v Nobby LANGFORD

SENTENCE

HIS HONOUR: Mr Langford, I am looking, of course, for the minimum appropriate sentence in respect of these two matters. In respect of the first matter the conclusion I have come to is that the appropriate penalty is a head sentence of four years and a non-parole period of eighteen months both to date from 10 August, 1986. In respect of the possession charge I impose a penalty of six months' imprisonment to date from 10 August 1986 and they are concurrent.

Briefly I could not have taken the course in relation to the non-parole period, which I regard as at the very bottom of the range, had it not been for the evidence of the detective who was satisfied you had no intention of firing at the relevant police officer . . . I am satisfied on your release you will not offend again and that you will become a useful member of the community.

Among the police documents relating to this part of Nobby's life, there is one saying that the factors relating to this last offence are similar to those surrounding his first major offence in June 1973, when he was seventeen. Back then he was also charged with firing at police to escape lawful apprehension, and attempted murder. But back then also, no one was murdered or maimed! And it was not my son who fired the gun anyway. But he still did six years' jail for that charge. He had now done the very same thing that he was supposed to have done all those years ago, but didn't! So where's the justice in that? Where is our hope? We live in such a depressing racist society. Back then, Nob served six years for something a white girl did. This time around, he really did fire at the police car, and he served eighteen months for it. HOW IRONIC! To be charged and re-charged for the same thing. How desperate my son must have been. How frustrated. How alone. Chewed up by the white laws of this colonial country.

The day Nobby was caught and charged—10 August 1986—was his dead brother David's birthday. He would have been 30 years old that day. In our Koori way there is no such thing as coincidence. The spirit forces make it happen. Like the first time I picked up a pen to write, 23 May 1984—30 years exactly after my grandfather, Sam Anderson the cricketer, died in 1959, aged 79—and he was still playing the game and scoring centuries! And after writing my first book, which took four and a half years and one near nervous breakdown from writing up all the hurts, I posted it away on 10 August 1987—David's birthday again. My granddaughter Stella was born on my dead daughter Pearl's birthday, 1 December. Stella is an absolute reincarnation of Pearl, even to the big black eyes, and hair, and long skinny frame. All these connections link us Koori mob up to our Dreaming. We are all connected in some way; this is our belief anyway.

DEPARTMENT OF CORRECTIVE SERVICES, N.S.W.
PARKLEA PRISON
PRISONER'S APPLICATION OR STATEMENT

21.8.87

From Prisoner: 143 Langford, N. 4 years
Expiry of Non-parole Period: 17.9.87
Due for Discharge: 24.5.89
Subject: Parole

Sirs,

I respectfully ask your compassionate consideration to granting me parole. The specific reasons for this request are:

To be able to undergo intensive sessions with my psychiatrist, Dr Kordick, to find the best way of handling my stress-related problems.

To relieve the great difficulty my family are experiencing

meeting the domestic and financial commitments of paying off our home.

I am confident of acquiring suitable and legal work whereby I can support my family with pride.

The pressures of working too many hours prevented me reporting as required. I have learnt a clear and valuable lesson by failing to report, and would like to assure you that this error will not be repeated.

As my records will confirm, I am capable of being a law-abiding citizen.

The sessions with Dr Kordick should teach me how to handle stress to prevent a recurrence again.

My wife and children's love and loyalty towards me is of such value that I would not ever jeopardize their peace and security again.

Respectfully,
Nobby Langford

Nobby wrote this story for Nicky when he and Anna lived at Woodvale Close, Plumpton in 1986.

Nikky's Story
Gordon Langford

For Nichole (Goodday my little Devil)

Here's a special little story for you, so mummy can read it to you before you go to sleep. It's about a little girl and her blanket. The little girl in the story is named Nikky, so really the story is about you.

No one is really sure when Nikky made friends with her blanket, but it was a very long time ago, because she couldn't say very much. Every time Nikky woke up she would get hold of her blanket and it was very hard to make her let go.

When she had her morning bath (which she enjoyed very much) she even wanted to take her blanket into the tub with her. And when she was being dressed, it was always difficult for mum because she had to put Nikky's clothes on while she was holding the blanket. Sometimes she would put her blanket over her head and pretend she was a ghost, and say, 'Ooh, Ooh, Ooh,' and frighten everyone. Then she would come out from under her blanket suddenly and laugh at her old dad who was scared of the 'ghosty'.

Every so often the blanket had to be washed because Nikky would drop milk and biscuits and dinner and chocolate and jelly beans all over it. Maybe she didn't drop these things by accident. She might have been feeding her blanket.

Anyway, when the blanket was in the washing machine, Nikky's mum had to watch her very carefully. Otherwise, she might have got into the washing machine also. Imagine what it would be like to be washed and spun-dried. Of course the blanket had to be spun-dried by the time Nikky went to bed, because without it she wouldn't go to sleep. And there was teddy and dolly and furry animals to think about. They couldn't go to sleep unless they were wrapped up in the blanket with Nikky too.

Every night when our two little children were fast asleep, mummy and daddy went from bed to bed to make sure their special chaps were nicely in and warm as toast, especially in winter, during weather when Jacky Frost is around, and as we tucked that blanket, that very special blanket under Nikky's chin, she would snuggle down until we could only see a mop of hair showing.

And that is the end of my story as I know it. I hope you liked hearing it. It made me happy to write it.

    Lots of love my dear Nikky,
    From Daddy

This was Nobby's first publication ever![2]

NEW SOUTH WALES GOVERNMENT
DEPARTMENT OF CORRECTIVE SERVICES

Psychological Report
8th July, 1987

Langford impressed me as a very concerned and anxious person who sincerely wanted to develop self awareness and methods of coping so that reoffending could be avoided and the quality of his day to day living improved . . .

Langford appears to have developed some control over his impulsiveness while in prison . . . This control he has developed appears to have stemmed in part from the motivation provided by his intense desire to retain his family and home. His control may also have been enhanced by increased ventilation of his feelings—he used to keep things bottled up thus worsening his mental state. It appears that Langford also responded well to counselling in this area and benefited from releasing his tensions through explaining his feelings. He appears to possess sufficient flexibility to modify his behaviour further so that he may become less tense in future . . . He reports he has used alcohol in the past to cope with stress and depression. He is aware that this is a destructive pattern which if continued would prevent him from meeting his goals . . .

Langford has maintained employment while in prison and has completed a Motor Maintenance Course by correspondence.

Departmental Psychiatric and Psychological reports did not indicate any psychiatric disturbance. However, these reports were from 1974. A report written in July 1987 by Dr. Barclay, an independent psychiatrist, described Langford's past behaviour . . . as indicative of a hysterical personality disorder . . . Throughout my sessions with Langford, his behaviour did not indicate the presence of psychiatric disturbance. However, his loss of control . . . and seemingly irrational thinking . . . may indicate a transient psychiatric disturbance precipitated by social

61

stresses. This suggests that his development of social skills may not be sufficient to prevent future episodes. This issue should be further explored and it would be advisable to have him monitored by a psychiatrist or psychologist while on parole.

Langford presents as a person who sincerely wants to organize his life and stay out of trouble. He seems to be most dedicated to his family and his home. He appears to have developed the incentive, the attitude and the control to attain his goals. I can see no benefit from his remaining in prison . . .

Kathleen Power
Psychologist
Parklea Prison

The time came for Nobby to front the court for his parole hearing. My daughter Pauline drove me and Michelle, my daughter-in-law, to court. We had to park in the judges' parking space in the Domain and behind the courts, Pauline hoping she wouldn't get a ticket! Nobby's lady, Anna, was waving to us. When we went inside the building, the courtroom was up a flight of stairs. By this time in my life, stairs weren't easy for me to climb.

I huffed and puffed my way up. Then we sat down and waited quietly as Nob was brought into the courtroom by two gungabuls, one on either side. After all the evidence was given by the police who'd charged him, they did say that he'd fired only at the radiator—which was *one* good thing. Then it was Nobby's turn to tell all about his traumas. His voice was so quiet. He was asked to speak louder. Then I glanced at all the parole people—four of them, all old, dignified, sedate people. They looked so grim and serious, and must have looked very frightening to my son. I was seated directly behind him, and when the parole board retired to consider their verdict, I whispered, 'Don't give up hope, son.'

'I won't, Mum,' he whispered back.

Then a hush fell over the courtroom, as the parole people came back in. Nobby stood up to face the judge, who told him, 'Your record is very bad. You've been in and out of trouble since your youth.'

With that, my heart sank, and Pauline and Anna took off outa the room. They didn't want to hear the bad news. But the judge rambled on and on. I was close to tears, thinkin, my God, they're not going to give Nob his parole. Then I heard the judge say to Nobby, 'The whole board voted unanimously that because of your work record, you are to be given another chance.' The tears fell outa my eyes then, and I wept unashamedly before the whole court. Everyone stood as the judge left the court.

Michelle took off down the stairs to tell Anna and Pauline, and I could hear Pauline's voice echoing up the stairway, 'Good one! Good one!' We kissed Nob goodbye. He'd be home for Christmas 1987, to share some time with all his mob.

Pauline did get that damn parking ticket after all, and she was lettin go with some obscenities and I said, 'Shut up Porkie Pie.' That's her nickname. 'You'll get pinched for bad language.'

Church bells were ringing as we drove off. 'Can you hear those church bells, Mum?' she asked. 'No, I can't hear a thing.' 'You must be gettin real deaf,' she said. 'I heard three bells' tolls' suppose to be a good omen, aye!' she added. I smiled to myself, I did hear them, real loud too! And knew they were bells ringing from our hearts!

5

THE SET-UP

While Nobby was in prison, Anna had stuck by him, going regularly to Parklea to visit him and taking the two little kids, Andy and Nichole. But after Nobby got outa Parklea, it wasn't too long before he and Anna broke up. So Nobby moved out and went to live with his sister Aileen, in Bidwill, Mt Druitt.

Anna was going through a divorce when she met Nobby, and she had never been involved with a person who'd had a police and jail record, so all this, combined with pressure about house payments, and she not being able to contribute because her children were asthmatics, added to their breakup. So they ended up separately but they both tried real hard to make the union work. And Nobby never saw the children anymore. He heard that Anna has since married again and lives in Melbourne.

When Nobby was living at Aileen's, he never had a car to get around in, so he sold his good lounge to a new Australian, for the princely sum of $300. This man needed a lounge, and Nobby needed a car to get around in, so fair exchange, no robbery.

A little while after he and Anna had broken up, Nobby went out for a few drinks one night, lookin for a bit of lovin, and ended up in the Kings Cross area. He engaged the services of a prostitute, and after they finished their sexual encounter, he paid her. Then he sat waiting in the car for his change, while she went off to get it. But she went into the brothel, rang the police, and claimed Nobby had threatened her with an axe for sexual favours. This was after they'd already had it! The police picked him up and bashed him. He was unconscious in the van. The police panicked and took him to hospital, where he woke up several hours later.

These police were from Kings Cross and they knew of Nobby's record. After all the revelations that came out of the Royal Commission into Police Corruption in New South Wales, I wonder now if those Kings Cross coppers were some of the ones that confessed to giving dope to prostitutes in return for favours for themselves, aye!

I was sitting in my little car in Bourke Street, Woolloomooloo, waiting for this woman to come back with my change, when all of a sudden the police were there and pulled me outa the car and something hit me on back of the head. I woke up in hospital with someone taking blood out of me, then I blacked out again and woke up in the police cell and was charged with raping, assaulting, and threatening these two prostitutes with an axe. All this was said to me while I was in the Sydney Police Centre cells with no clothes on. I had no clothes on. I couldn't walk properly because I was all bruised and battered.

While Nobby was in the hospital he was examined by a doctor appointed by the police. He was also examined by a doctor I got hold of from the Aboriginal Medical Service. The two doctors' reports were very different. Makes ya wonder, aye!

NEW SOUTH WALES POLICE

Statement in matter of: Nobby Langford
Place: Sydney Hospital
Date: 22 March, 1988.
Name: Dr. Stephen K. C———
Occupation: Medical Practitioner —— STATES:-

I am aware that if I sign this statement and any part of this statement is untrue to my knowledge, I may be liable to punishment.

1. I, Stephen K. C———, hereby certify as follows:-
. . . At 0510 Hours on Thursday 17th March, 1988, I attended a male patient named Nobby Langford who presented to this hospital following an apparent collapse and unconsciousness in a Police van.

2. I examined the patient and did not find any evidence of any injury to his head, chest, abdomen, pelvis and limbs, nor any abnormality of his cardiovascular, respiratory, gastrointestinal and central nervous systems.

3. The patient exhibited no objective evidence of the effects of drugs or alcohol.

4. No apparent injuries were sustained. Urine and drug samples were sent to St. Vincent's Hospital and following analysis these samples were negative for paracetamol and inhaled substances.

5. Initially at the time of admission of the patient, he was placid and not responding to pain. At 0700 hours the patient woke up and began to swear and spit.

6. At 0735 hours on Thursday 17 March, 1988, the patient was released into the custody of Police.

I declare no part of this statement to be untrue to my knowledge.

I am aware that it may be used in legal proceedings. It accurately sets out the evidence that I would be prepared to give, if necessary, as a court witness.

SIGNATURE: K.S.C——

WITNESS: J.B——
22 March, 1988

ABORIGINAL MEDICAL SERVICE CO-OPERATIVE LTD.

36 Turner Street,
Redfern, NSW, 2016

28.4.88

Re: *Nobby Langford visit on 17.3.88*

I was asked to visit this man at Sydney Police Centre on 17.3.88. There were two main issues of concern to me. These were that he was in a depressed mental state and talked of suicide and also that he had marks on his body consistent with a recent assault. He had visible bruising to the anterior chest wall and he had abrasions to the left wrist. His ankles had been shaven and he showed the marks of having had an intravenous catheter inserted into the veins about the ankle. I was not able to physically examine him fully as he was separated from me by the glass screen of the interview room. He told me that these injuries had been sustained after arrival at the Police station. I felt he required no treatment for these injuries. I talked with him about his feelings of despair and possible suicide and formed the impression that he was not immediately suicidal, but that a significant risk existed. I made recommendations to the officer in charge of the cells that a close eye be kept on him in a normal cell. I also recommended that he be given urgent priority to be moved to a proper Remand Centre at the earliest opportunity if he was to be held in custody. I understand that he was moved to Long Bay on the next day.

Yours sincerely,
S. C. W—— M.B. Ch.B.
MEDICAL OFFICER

Dr C——, the police doctor, couldn't explain why I was unconscious on the table—unless he'd said I got bashed on the head with a lump of wood or something (which is more to the truth). But we can't say that can we!

Detective James A. B—— was the main body responsible for arresting me in March 1988 for allegedly raping and abducting two Kings Cross prostitutes. I deny all charges which is why I went to trial. James A. B—— was great mates with Daryl B——, the guy I was charged with firing shots at in 1973. It was known that Daryl B—— hated me and William S——'s guts, because we were supposed to have fired at them in 1973. James A. B—— squared up for Daryl B—— when he arrested me in 1988. Daryl B—— is high and mighty now, a crown sergeant or somethin in relation to transport in the police dept.

It's now May 1996, and I've got a newspaper clipping in front of me saying that James A. B—— is currently under investigation by the police corruption inquiry. Nobby always said the police hated him because of his charges for firing at police in the first instance. They do not tolerate anyone standing up against them.

Maybe in the long run the facts will all come out. Who knows, maybe when I'm dead and gone they'll probably say 'I'm sorry for the amount of jail that you've done.' I hope you get ya right whack Daryl B——, you bastard.

While Nob was in jail waiting for his trial, I received this letter from him:

Darling mother,

I'm sorry I've not written for quite a while. I'm just so pissed off with being back in this shit hole. You know if these charges stick I'm going to be doing a long sentence. I wouldn't feel so bad if I'd done what they say I did. But I'm telling you Mum, I didn't do it. I would never do what they say I did. Maybe the cops gave those bitches some heroin to set me up.

I guess I've adjusted pretty quickly to being back in jail. I feel like I've been in one jail or another for most of my life. When I found myself in a man's jail for the very first time when I was 17, it was a very rude awakening—to being a man. Jail is the absolute pits. It's a dump. It is the most depressing, dehumanising place in the world. They treat you like a piece of shit. And you got to mind your business, don't talk out of school—there's so many different things you've gotta learn.

Anyway baby, thank you for sending that money. It will help a real lot. You wouldn't believe the art I can do. Especially my painting, I've managed to get some oil paints and I've got a couple of pieces of masonite, and you wouldn't believe what I can do with paint and brushes. I've just finished one of a horseman bringing a pregnant filly out of the ice. I'm calling it 'The Foal' and some bloke here wants to buy it off me. But being my first painting I'm going to keep it for you, OK. I'm going to sign off for now and I'll try and write to you before the weekend. I love you.

Nobby XXX

Pam Johnston was the jail art teacher who encouraged Nobby with his art while in Long Bay in 1989, and she also helped him with his first art show, being involved in first Koori Perspecta at Art Space in 1989. Later, when he was in Berrima, they became an item, but it finished when he was discharged in June 1993—mostly because of two artists' different temperaments.

I travelled to Gosford with Pam for Nobby's trial, and it took nearly all day. I gave evidence, but was feeling like the pack was stacked against my son again.

A lot of evidence was not produced at the trial in Gosford. The two prostitutes were seen by a crown sergeant at Gosford police station during the intermission at lunch time, half way through the trial, standing there talking, going arm in arm for lunch. And it's well known throughout the legal system that two witnesses at the one trial are not allowed to say anything to each other or anybody else in relation to that trial. These two ladies were seen by the crown sergeant who never came forward. If he had've the trial would have been aborted. My legal bloke asked the crown sergeant to give evidence, but he didn't want to jeopardise his position.

It was about four o'clock when the jury came in with their verdict—guilty! It took them only one hour to decide this; even before they went in to deliberate they were all watching their clocks, checking the time. After the trial, me and Pammy cried all the way back to Sydney. He was sentenced to eight years' jail with five years' non-parole period, serving five years three months.

You can be put off, murdered in jail, set up by the screws—the horrendous stories you read about in the papers are true.

But these days, it's better for this mob in jail compared to how it was years ago. The Bathurst riot did that. The Bathurst riot boys—some of them got killed, got crippled, bashed half to death by baton-wielding screws—these blokes made it better for blokes in prisons today. There was nothing in jail when I was a kid. There were no TVs and no radios. Just a little Saturday and Sunday night two hour radio broadcast. Virtually you had nothing. You had a bit of education. But you can't sort of sit there reading a fucking book all night. You need to do something else. But in the end after the Royal Commission into the Bathurst riot, things did change in jail. Things got more lenient because they got rid of all the old bashers, the screws, the ones that used to kick into crims—the Grafton clique of screws who used to bash into the crims. And the mod squad used to bash the fuck out of ya. You'd wake up in another jail. I could go on and on. Anyway the Bathurst riot boys changed jails for the better. You got better tobacco, decent soap. You were allowed to buy shampoo, and day-to-day hygiene—you could get jockettes and new socks, the sort of things that would stop disease in the long run. For the changes for the better that happened in jail, you can thank the Bathurst boys and my hat goes off to you, because you suffered probably more than I'll ever know.

After Nobby's trial, he was sent back to Long Bay. He applied for a classification to go to Berrima Jail, and after waiting eight months, he got it. The reason he wanted to change was that there was a German art teacher in residence at Berrima and Nobby wanted to learn to do portraiture. He could already do some of the traditional art styles, but now he wanted to be able to paint people's faces.

Nobby's letters stirred up every sad and painful emotion in me. Some of them tore the guts outa me.

Darling Mother,

I'm so proud of everything you've achieved. I've not been a perfect son to you. Maybe I inherited my mother's bad temper.

Even though I have done some things that have made you proud of me, I could have tried a lot harder. I could have been a lot easier to get along with, and been more tolerant of other people. I'm gonna start writing a book about my experiences in jail. I've enclosed an article Joe gave me about the racist Ruxton. Don't worry, you will be getting some paintings soon.

Love Nobby XXXX

This is the letter from Joe, another inmate, about some racist remarks by Bruce Ruxton.

15th October 1988

I'm a 5ft 7 Maltese who has lived in your country for the last 28 years. I have endured insults, racism and bigotry from our Anglo-Saxon friends right from the beginning. I'm sure this sounds very familiar to you as you've been copping the same for the last 200 years. I truly believe that everybody is equal regardless of origin, colour and belief, and the sooner the world wakes up to this simple truth the better it will be. But of course the oppressors will put up a hell of a fight before letting some of their powers be rightfully shared.

My main aim in this country is to interest people in my cause to get the Australian Constitution changed to include the UN Bill of Rights which guarantees the freedom of ethnic people to speak their language, freedom of religion, etc. There's no point calling this country democratic if these basic human rights are not constitutionally binding. The United Nations did ask Australia in the early 80s to start implementing this procedure but the move was defeated in the Senate! And they call this a free country. What a bloody joke! However sooner or later they will have to admit that there are other people apart from Anglo-Saxons living, paying taxes, and contributing to this country, who must enjoy the same constitutional rights. It makes me sick listening to the Liberal Party, the RSL (Bruce Ruxton), and the new chief bigot, Ron Casey. Surely these bigoted racists have no place in your country. They are bent on keeping the white Protestant blue-eyed blonde Aussie image.

They will find excuses to hate everybody, maybe they should be exported to the USA to join the Ku Klux Klan. I'm 1000% against racism both as a Catholic and a human being. That's my stand. Do me a favour, Ruby, and never loose your sense of humour.

Your friend Joe

What a beautiful letter from someone who's not from this country but has been treated with the same racism we Kooris put up with every day of our lives. Makes ya wonder, doesn't it?

Another letter from Nobby said:

Mother I'm not too happy as you can imagine. I got your letter today. Not much to tell you, only that I'm in the horrors about being locked up again! Every time I seem to start getting myself together something always happens. The gungies must hate me! Tell my family that I'm sorry. Send Pat's address and ask Aileen to look after my things. Ask her to pick up my wallet for me as my licence and my glasses are at the cop shop. I'm gonna start writing my story soon, hope it turns out a good yarn like yours.

Love you, Mum,
Nobby XXX

Soon Nobby was writing me:

Mum, I've started the book. I called it 'Haunted by the Past'—what do ya think, Mum? I have to save up for a television as the art teachers here at Long Bay don't seem too interested in my art, maybe it's because I'm black who knows?

After reading through all these letters I was so overcome that I cried, tears welling up and wetting my glasses and I thanked the Good Spirit of our Aboriginal Dreamtime for looking after him in the place he called a shit hole. Nobby never did finish that book. He tossed that ball to me. So look who's doin it now! 'Mum, you write the stories,' he said, 'and I'll paint the history.'

6

BLACK DEATHS IN CUSTODY

While Nobby was doing this long stretch in jail, the Royal Commission into Black Deaths in Custody was going on. Even before the official inquiry I was always worried about Nobby when he was in jail. I received a letter from him that stated: 'Mum, if I ever go back to jail again, they'll bring me out feet first because bein locked up like an animal and bein told by screws, do this do that, it's nearly drivin me mad! I can't take it anymore.' The pressure was so bad. And Nobby was very depressed from time to time. It really got me down. I was always worried that he would have survived the police, the wardens and the other inmates, but then take his own life.

But he has survived. Not everyone has been so lucky.

During the time Nobby was in jail, David Gundy was shot during a police raid on his home in 1989. I remembered back to the time when Nob was on the run in 1974 after breaking out of Long Bay. Just like in the Gundy case, the police burst into Dianne's home looking for Nobby, with their guns drawn. I was quoted in the newspapers at the time pleading, 'Don't shoot my son down like a mad dog.' David Gundy's shooting easily could have happened to my son.

The *Encyclopedia of Aboriginal Australia* describes David Gundy's death this way:

> Shortly before 6am on 27 April 1989, eight members of the NSW police Special Weapons and Operations Section (SWOS) smashed in the door of Gundy's home and burst into his bedroom. He was shot in the chest at close range with a shotgun. Suffering massive injuries, he died almost immediately. The attack on his home had been one of six simultaneous raids mounted in the hope of capturing John Porter, an ex-prisoner suspected of shooting two policemen, one of whom had died. Porter was a casual acquaintance of the Gundy family . . . .
>
> A coronial inquest found simply that Gundy had died accidentally and an internal police department investigation found that complaints about SWOS actions made by members of the public in petitions to the ombudsman could not be sustained. At this point J.H. Wootten, commissioner of the Royal Commission into Aboriginal Deaths in Custody, included Gundy's death among the many the Commission was investigating. The NSW government opposed this, on the grounds that Gundy had not been in police custody when killed, and in April 1990 successfully took action in the Federal Court to restrain Wootten. Wootten successfully appealed this decision. His 315-page report on Gundy's death is a condemnation of the police handling of the case.[1]

The police were reluctant to recognise the shortcomings in the training methods of SWOS, and the unlawfulness of their raid on Gundy's home. Instead, they sought to denigrate and blame David Gundy for what happened, although he was in truth a law-abiding, hard-working family man. The killing of this man was followed by an assassination of his character.

Ms Dolly Eates, David Gundy's wife, said she believed that Gundy died because he was an Aboriginal person, and that he was killed in retaliation for the police officer that was shot by John Porter, who was an islander. The SWOS, which called itself the 'elite of the elite', was totally discredited.

Why is it that police have had such a big role in the oppression of and violence against Aboriginal people? It goes back to colonial times when the police performed tasks that in other countries were carried out by the army. John O'Sullivan's *Mounted Police in NSW* says that this is why 'the Australian police were inevitably involved in actions that departed widely from the standards of legality observed . . . by police in England.'[2] The police here were the front line in an undeclared land war. Until 1992, white law did not recognise prior Aboriginal ownership of this country. Therefore any Aboriginal defence of land was classified as a crime. Aboriginal people defending their land were moved off, arrested or shot by police as lawbreakers—a practice known as 'dispersal'.

The Anti-Discrimination Board's 1982 *Study of Street Offences by Aborigines* states that 'the first contact that Aborigines had with police was as the force of dispossession and, in some instances, the dispensers of summary justice and the instigators of massacres.' The police were officially the 'guardians' of Aboriginal people, distributing rations, clothing, and protection. But 'the dominant role of the police was to be the "prosecutor" rather than "protector".'[3] They removed fair-skinned Aboriginal children from their families, controlled Aboriginal people by withholding rations, and shifted whole communities off their lands. Maybe the police who killed David Gundy and who harassed my son are still haunted by memories of their colonial past.

I want to write about some of the Aboriginal deaths in custody. The lives of any one of these could easily have been my son Nobby's. I feel that now is the time to show people what really happened. Maybe it will open up people's eyes! It knocks the guts outa me to write it up, so you read it, and form your own opinions. For legal reasons I haven't been able to include all the facts as I know them, or write about all the people who have died. I have had to cut back some details I think you all should know. That's the white fella's law for you, aye?

CASE 1: EDDIE MURRAY[4]

Eddie Murray, a popular, happy-go-lucky, 21-year-old, was picked up for drunkenness by police in the NSW country town of Wee Waa on 12 June 1981. Within one hour he was dead. He was found hung in his cell by a piece of prison blanket, his knees slightly bent and his feet touching the floor. Eddie's blood alcohol level at the time of his death was 0.3%. At the inquest into Eddie's death, police agreed that he was so drunk he couldn't scratch himself, yet Eddie is supposed to have torn a strip off a prison blanket, deftly folded it and threaded it through the bars of the ventilation window of his cell, tied two knots, then fashioned a noose and hung himself while standing with his feet on the floor. There was no chair in the cell for him to stand on.

Police testimony conflicted with the evidence of four Aboriginal witnesses who saw Fitzgerald in the police van that had been used to pick up Murray. Police witnesses said he was not in the van.

The coroner recorded an open verdict on the death. He found that Eddie Murray had died by hanging, at the hand of person or persons unknown. The coroner said there was no evidence that Eddie had taken his own life, but that he could, even while drunk, have formed a noose. He said that the expert witnesses agreed that it was possible, though improbable, for a person with such a high blood alcohol level to decide to hang himself and to do so. The coroner said he could find no evidence that an offence was committed by any person and therefore he would not submit the inquest papers to the Attorney General.

Eddie's death came as the last straw for his family. Eddie's father, Arthur, had campaigned to get better working conditions for Aboriginal cotton workers, and was detested by many whites in the town. 'Sometimes I thought we were living in the Deep South in America,' he said. After Eddie's death, the Murray family moved out of Wee Waa.

When Eddie's mother visited his grave with Mr Justice Muirhead from the Royal Commission, they found that the grave had been desecrated. Someone had roughly etched the word 'HUNG' into the stone crucifix marking Eddie's grave. The headstone of Eddie's sister's grave had also been pushed over.

CASE 2: JOHN PAT[5]

On the night of 28 September, 1983, sixteen-year-old John Pat was found dead in a police cell in the West Pilbara town of Roebourne, WA. Earlier that night, five off-duty police had got into a fight with a group of John Pat's friends outside the Roebourne pub. He had stepped in to try and help his friends. He was later dragged to the police station as he was unconscious and couldn't walk. He received no medical attention. Later it was found he had two broken ribs and he had received at least ten blows to the head as well as being kicked. He would not have survived without major surgery as he also had a torn aorta.

Seven months later, an all-white jury acquitted the five police officers who had been charged with manslaughter. After the inquiry, the police concerned were exonerated and reinstated to their previous positions.

I think this is a good place to include a poem written about John Pat by our old warrior-author Jack Davis:

'John Pat'

(Dedicated to Maisie Pat, and to all mothers who have suffered similar loss.)

Right of life
the pious said
forget the past
the past is dead.
But all I see
in front of me
is a concrete floor
a cell door
and John Pat.
Agh! Tear out the page
forget his age
thin skull they cried
that's why he died!
But I can't forget
the silhouette
of a concrete floor
a cell door
and John Pat.
The end product
of Guddia law
is a viaduct
for fang and claw
and a place to dwell

like Roebourne's hell
of a concrete floor
a cell door
and John Pat.
He's there—where?
There in their minds now
deep within,
there to prance
a sidelong glance
a silly grin
to remind them all
of a Guddia wall
a concrete floor
a cell door
and John Pat.

CASE 3: ROBERT WALKER[6]

'Solitary Confinement'[7]
Robert Walker

Have you ever been ordered to strip
Before half a dozen barking eyes,
Forcing you against a wall—
ordering you to part your legs, and bend over?
Have you ever had a door slammed
Locking you out of the world,
Propelling you into timeless space—
To the emptiness of silence?
Have you ever laid on a wooden bed—
In regulation pyjamas,
And tried to get a bucket to talk—
In all seriousness?
Have you ever begged for blankets
From an eye staring through a hole in the door,

Rubbing at the cold air digging into your flesh—
Biting down on your bottom lip, while mouthing
'Please, Sir'?
Have you ever heard screams in the middle of the night,
Or the sobbings of a stir crazy prisoner,
Echo over and over again in the darkness—
Threatening to draw you into its madness?
Have you ever rolled up into a human ball
And prayed for sleep to come?
Have you ever laid awake for hours
Waiting for morning to mark yet another day of being
alone?
If you've never experienced even one of these,
Then bow your head and thank God.
For it's a strange thing indeed—
This rehabilitation system!

Robert Joseph Walker died between 4.30 and 5 am on Tuesday, 28 August 1984, while a prisoner in Fremantle Prison, WA. Robert was 25 years old and was doing time, like so many of his people, in a state where the fact that Aboriginal people make up 3% of the total population and never less than ten times that proportion of the jail population is a direct reflection of the colonial oppression which Robert suffered in his short life and death.

The story of Robert Walker's death is one of the stories I wanted to write about, because I think you all should know about it. But, because of the law I can only give you the bare bones of the case. Sometimes I feel like I can't win. How are people going to know what happens to our people if we can't tell it like we see it?

At 4 o'clock on that fatal morning, prison officers went to move Robert from his cell, after noticing he had cut his wrists. Robert emerged on the landing outside his cell and saw a prison officer with a gun. He screamed, 'They're goin to kill me! Murder! Murder!' At this point, other prisoners awakened and witnessed what they described as a 'brutal awful assault' on Robert.

At 5.15 am, Dr David Brockman, the prison doctor, pronounced that Robert was dead. The first official statements were not forthcoming until some twelve hours after the death. The Prisons Department put out stories in the mainstream press, first of suicide, then of a Largactil overdose, and then on 1-2 September, they said a 'mystery illness' was the cause of death. The press backed these stories.

A post mortem was conducted on the day of the death by Dr Pocock. Dr Pocock did not find the cause of death.

Linda Walker, Robert's mother, who lived in South Australia, heard of her son's death on the radio, and got some official explanations. She battled for a week for permission to have a second independent autopsy conducted on the body of her son, and the body returned to the family for burial. The WA Prisons Department initially refused her requests, and tried to arrange for the cremation of the body.

Finally, a second autopsy was conducted in Adelaide and found Robert had suffered 'acute brain death, due to an obstruction of the blood supply to the brain caused by compression of the neck.'

At the inquest it was found that death arose by way of 'misadventure'.

After the inquest, the prison officers' union issued a statement in the press saying they were considering legal action against the 41 prisoner witnesses who testified about Robert's death.

CASE 4: CHARLIE MICHAELS[8]

On 9 October 1984 at 10.30 pm, Dr Allan Newman, Medical Officer for Barton Mill Prison in WA, received a phone call informing him of a prisoner's death. Prior to this call, Charlie Michaels, prisoner of Barton Mill Prison, was flat on his face with four prison officers kneeling on him and pinning down his arms and legs. Charlie Michaels was soon in handcuffs and an officer's trouser belt was tied around his ankles. Then the prisoner's own belt was used to lash his hands from behind, to his feet. A standard issue baton used as a windlass was twisted around the belt, tightening the belt until his hands almost touched his feet. The prison officers later claimed that even this form of restraint, which is apparently in line with the WA Prison Department regulations, did not work, and so the officers struggled with the prisoner. They later estimated that the struggle, in the narrow doorway of a cramped office lasted about 40 minutes.

The wardens alleged that it started with a depressed and rambling Michaels, who was said to be a quiet prisoner who made little trouble, grabbing the lapels of Superintendent Stan Lodge's jacket. The struggle ended with Michaels' death. His crumpled and restrained body became a testament to life behind bars for Aboriginals.

The Perth City Coroner found that Charlie Michaels had died of a heart attack. Dr Newman, the Prison Medical Officer, stated at the Coroners Court, 'I believe that the effect of struggling almost certainly precipitated a major cardiac arhythmia which resulted in his immediate death.' The same court was also told that Charlie Michaels had no previous medical record of heart problems. The WA Prison Department Superintendent, Dr David Brockman, said that Charlie Michaels, at 31 years old, suffered from diabetes, but was otherwise healthy. Mr Rob Riley, the then

National Aboriginal Conference Chairperson, and Mr Ivan Yarran, Aboriginal Legal Service President, criticised the circumstances of Charlie Michaels' death. They pointed out that if Michaels died of a heart attack, as was alleged, it was strange that no medical aid was given. Contrary to the WA government's assurances that adequate and timely assistance was available to all prisoners, Michaels' death proved otherwise. Aboriginal people, and in particular Michaels' relatives, were not satisfied with the government's statement on the matter. Western Australia has the worst record in the nation for imprisonment of Aboriginals: the rate is twice as high as that of any other state.

CASE 5: TONY KING[9]

Tony King died on 31 October, 1985. He was a Maori man, originally named Tony Majurey, and was married to an Aboriginal woman, Carmen Culbong, so he was part of the Aboriginal community. His sister-in-law worked for the National Aboriginal Conference, and King and his wife helped her with her work.

For six years prior to Tony's death, police had been trying in vain to solve a number of rapes occurring in and around the town of Geraldton, WA. A long and expensive operation was conducted and because of the high public profile of the crimes, the police were under enormous pressure to catch 'the Geraldton rapist'. Finally, their operation was stepped up with long nights of police foot patrols and officers hiding in shadowy laneways to surprise the rapist. On 31 October 1985, Tony King happened to be in the patrolled area. He was chased and brought to the ground. He died soon after. The police were acquitted of responsibility for Tony King's death in the coronial inquest.

The pathologist, Dr Pocock, reported that King had died of 'asphyxiation', compression of the chest, and coronary atherosclerosis (hardening of the arteries). There is no evidence that Tony King had ever been sought by police as a suspect for the Geraldton rapes. Family members commented that after Tony's death: 'The police thought he would be the perfect scapegoat for the rapes they could not solve.'

Immediately following Tony's death, Detective Sergeant Brandis, who had headed the rape inquiry for the past two years at Geraldton CIB, announced that: 'The police have no conclusive evidence at this stage that the deceased man was the Geraldton rapist.' Yet a barrage of media articles appeared, claiming that the rapist had been caught.

Few newspapers, if any, bothered to criticise the death of another black man while in police custody in WA. The heat was taken off this issue by the media ensuring the public had no sympathy for a dead 'rapist' who police were under pressure to catch. The trial by media continued with purely circumstantial evidence being released. The police, however, began to lose face when they continually refused to release what they called their 'irresistible inference', on which their claims, that King was the Geraldton rapist, were based. Eventually, police were forced to release it. They did this after the due date and not in accordance with ground rules set for its release. It was still, however, only circumstantial evidence, much of which would have been inadmissable if Tony had been alive to face their allegations in court.

The Perth City Coroner handed down his finding at the coronial inquest, finding that King's death was caused by 'misadventure'. He said that: 'Where death arises in the performance of a lawful act and there is no intention to bring about such an event, then death is said to be a result of "misadventure".'

King's grieving family are still fighting to clear his name.

CASE 6: DIXON GREEN[10]

Dixon Green was from Kununurra in far north Western Australia. He died in Broome Regional Prison on 19 November 1985. An autopsy conducted by a government pathologist concluded that his death was the result of a heart attack.

Dixon Green's family and friends demanded that a second post mortem be carried out by a forensic pathologist. Unfortunately, there was no forensic pathologist in private practice in Western Australia, and neither the Greens nor the Aboriginal Legal Service had funds to fly a pathologist from interstate.

It seems that when an independent post mortem was done, only skin specimens were used. The independent pathologist had no access to the body.

On 5 April 1986, at an inquest into Dixon Green's death, the Derby Coroner, Paul Heaney, ruled that there was no evidence of violence. He found that death was by natural causes. This put an official end to the case. At the inquest, Dr Kevin Coleman, of the North Australian Aboriginal Medical Service, told how when he was called to Broome Regional Prison on the night Dixon died, he found him still slumped on the toilet. No attempt had been made to resuscitate him.

The Green family don't believe that Dixon died from natural causes: 'My brother had no record of heart trouble, and neither has my family,' says Ken Green. 'He exercised every day and we don't believe he had a drinking problem.

We aren't going to believe what the Prison Department says, because there's been too many "heart attacks" in jail.'

CASE 7: DANIEL YOCK[11]

On 7 November 1993, Daniel Yock, an eighteen-year-old Aboriginal youth, was taken into custody by police on a South Brisbane street, and died shortly afterwards. He was locked in the back of a police paddy wagon and was dead on arrival at the city police watch-house.

Later that evening, six police were brought together for a so called 'counselling session'. They had four hours to prepare their evidence prior to formal interviews with senior police in the early hours of the morning of 8 November.

The central issue in the inquiry into Daniel Yock's death ... the claim that Yock died suddenly of an extremely rare, undiagnosed and undetectable 'stroke. The Aboriginal Legal Service formally requested the Criminal Justice Commission's (CJC) inquiry and is responsible for its outcome. Daniel Yock was the 52nd Aborigine to die in custody in the four years since the 1989 cut-off date of the Royal Commission. The rate of killing has increased among Aboriginal and non-Aboriginal prisoners since the Government's Royal Commission into Black Deaths in Custody.

The day after Daniel's death, angry demonstrators marched on the police watch-house chanting 'No CJC' and 'Murderers'. But on the same day, after a closed-door meeting which included Aboriginal Legal Service president Sam Watson, and senior police, the CJC formally took over the official investigation of Daniel Yock's death. On 12 November, the CJC announced a public inquiry under Commissioner Lewis Wyvill, one of the Federal Labor government's Royal Commissioners into Aboriginal deaths in custody.

'Battle Heroes'[12]
Graeme Dixon

You bucked an evil system
putting up a hell of a fight
struggling brave and hard
against the captors' aggressive spite.
So they savagely beat your bodies
whilst chained to the ground.
For what logical reason?
Because your skin was brown!
Though the body's strength was sapped
ancient spirits fought on
so fragile throats were compressed
till all signs of life had gone.
Other mortal injuries from battle
severe enough to cause death
cracked the head!
bullet hole!
strangulation!
all took away life's sweet breath
State paid doctors and police
ruled against you of course!
Coming to neutral judgements
'reasonable bloody force!'
And this informed Nyoongah people
the state sanctions this war
so fight in self defence
you're not protected by Queen's law.
Though they lost this battle
warriors brave and bold
the survivors will not rest
till injustice has been resolved
for *'all is fair in love and war'*
is the invaders' battle-cry.

So defy this oppression
or we're all destined to die.
And Yagan* is still the hero
pioneer of our righteous cause
(will always be remembered
with respectful, silent pause).
But there's a new breed of martyr
who in bloody battle fell
Maori Tony, Robert and Charlie
John Pat and young Ricky as well.

* Yagan—an Aboriginal freedom fighter

7

NOBBY'S RELEASE, 1993

We decided months before that, on the day that Nobby was gonna be released from Berrima Jail, Jeffery and I would go and fetch him. My youngest daughter, Pauline, arranged a car from Thrifty Car Rentals. None of our bomb cars could go the distance. We couldn't go to pick the man up in one of those, could we? I had planned with Jeffery to pick me up at Granville on the day before Nob's release, and stay the night at his place in Claymore in the suburb of Campbelltown, in Sydney's south-west.

Jeffrey set the alarm for five o'clock, and we were up and dressed and ready to roll at half-past six. I noticed as we sped along that my young son was enjoying this trip in this near new Commodore. I was thinking, how odd—it was a white car, and would soon be filled with us black-fellas!

We arrived at Berrima at half-past seven: too early. Nobby had warned us that they don't open the big gate to let inmates out before eight o'clock. So we sat and listened to the radio. Jeffery said, 'Gee Ma, I'll bet he's rushing around like a cat on hot bricks.'

'Yeah, I'll bet he damn well is. Ya know how much of a panic merchant he is.'

Next thing we heard a piercing whistle—

PHWWWEEETTT—and looking towards the big gate we saw him waving to us to pull the car in. Next thing we were cuddling and hugging each other as if we'd never let him go.

First thing he asked for was his bloody licence. 'Give me a chance to get it outa me handbag, son,' I said, handing it to him.

He laughingly took it saying, 'Jeffo, I'm gonna drive, Bra,' and he turned to the screws lookin on and told them, 'I'm legal,' flashin his licence. Then the boys loaded on all his personal belongings and his paintings. There were boxes and boxes, everywhere.

'Mum, looks like there's no room for you in the car,' he said. 'We'll have ta leave ya here at Berrima.'

'Like bloody hell!' I retorted, hardly able to control my gigglin in front of the screws who were keepin a watchful eye on all the packing.

Nob shook hands with these men. They regarded him as a good inmate, as he'd earned their respect. He was the 'activity crim', who distributed material for crafts, artwork or hobbies here, and had more keys than the damn screws!

Before we left Nobby said, 'We have to wait, Mum, until my boss man comes, so as we can go into the back of the jail. I've got a surprise for you, OK?'

We had to wait for about ten minutes, until we saw a big prison van drive past us waving for us to follow, and we turned into the side street that led us to the back of the jail.

There was a big wood fire burnin where some prisoners were warming themselves as it was damn cold. As we alighted from the car, these prisoners came forward to shake Nobby's hand, wishing him well, and saying to me, 'Don't let him come back here any more, missus.'

One of the fellows was carryin something wrapped up in a cloth and he handed it to Nobby, who shook his hand saying, 'Thanks mate.' Then we left that depressing place with its high walls and restricted boundaries with razor wire all around the perimeter.

Outside again, Nobby handed me the article wrapped in the cloth. 'Go on Mum, open it, it's ya present. That mate of mine made it for you.' I unwrapped it hurriedly, wondering what it could be. Tears ran down outa my eyes when I took the cloth off: it was a sculpture of the face of my eldest daughter Pearl. She'd made history in 1968 by being the first Aboriginal to dance with an Australian prime minister, but she'd died the year after at age seventeen. I was so overwhelmed to see her face again; it was beautiful.

'How did he do this?' I asked Nobby.

'I gave him sister Pearl's photo to work from.'

Nobby gunned the motor of the car. 'This is a deadly car, Jeffo. How about playing some tapes?'

As we sped along the highway towards Mittagong, I sat content, revelling in the joy. After all these years I had my only two sons that were left with me in this car, making a fast getaway from Berrima Jail. I glanced at them—my two sons: Jeffery with his long hair flying in the wind, singing at the top of his voice in tune with the tape and beating out the drum beats on the dashboard of the car. Nobby was lettin go, singin too, tryin to drown Jeffery out. I chuckled to myself. It made my heart glow with pride, just listening to them sharing this special moment together.

As we pulled up behind Jeffery's house, his two little girls, Jessie and Samantha, ran to meet us and hugged their Uncle Nobby. Then they asked if he had any lollies.

The boys unloaded the television and the beautiful hand-made chess table that Debbie, David's wife, had bought from the craft centre there at Berrima when she was visiting Nobby. Shellie, Jeffery's wife, made coffee and we all sat around yarnin. Nobby was spoiling baby Zelina who was crawling all over the place.

Nobby opened his wallet and, counting all his money, gave half to Jeffery. Jeffo was on the dole and battling, so this made him smile up big. One of my adopted sons, Allo, then came in with his little family, and the boys reminisced over coffee about long gone days. Nobby couldn't get over all the grand-kids. 'Youse are all leaving me for dead with all these kids ya got. Looks like I have to get crackin to get a couple of my own before I get too old!'

Everybody agreed with that. 'Ya better hurry up, Nobby. You're missing out on all the fun—dirty nappies and getting up in the middle of the night, making bottles and changing chukka bums.' They were all laughing and having a go at him.

The boys had bought six tinnies and offered one to Nobby in celebration of his homecoming, but he shook his head. 'Booze never got me anywhere, only into all the trouble I've been in. No thanks!'

We said our goodbyes to Shellie and the kids and headed over to my other adopted son Patrick's place at Campbelltown. As we drove away I was thinking, gee, this is only a small part of all this mob of mine, and when they all got together, lookout!—much fun and happiness.

Jeffery went back home with Allo, and me and Nobby were off to Woolloomooloo. Pammy girl had planned a lunch for him. Nobby was gonna be staying at Pammy's for a while to see how they went. Although these two had had a thing going for the five and a half years he'd been behind bars, they'd never had a relationship on the outside.

Driving along, Nobby said, 'This place has changed a lot since I've been away. There's expressways all over the place now, coming and going into the city.'

But as we got further towards the city, he said to me, 'Mum, I want to go out to the cemetery to the graves first.'

His voice had gone real quiet. He'd never been there since we'd buried David in December of 1984, nine years earlier. The closer we got to Botany Cemetery the more I could sense the tension in him. So many people he loved had been taken from him, like a piece of his heart torn away. The loss showed in his face.

At the cemetery, I directed him, pointing out where his uncle Kevin was buried. Then as we drove down the hill, I pointed to a huge blue headstone. 'Ya see that blue headstone? That's where brother Bill and David are—just in front of that.' At the bottom of the roadway we turned right, and I showed him where to pull up just in front of Dad and Pearl's grave. Getting outa the car, I said 'This is sister Pearl's and your grandfather's, my Dad's grave. I had to bury Pearl on top of Dad; I couldn't raise enough money for her own plot.'

'Mum, why do people have to die?'

'We are all born to die, son. Everything that lives and breathes is born to die. Nothing lasts forever.'

I sat on the side of Dad and Pearl's grave and said, 'I'll wait here, OK?'

I sat and talked to my Dad and Pearly, saying, 'Look after all our loved ones out here. We'll be all together one day in our Koori Dreamtime.' Glancing up the hill towards where Nobby was, I could see him wiping his eyes. I knew he needed to be with his brothers and talk to them too.

When he came back to me he said, 'I'll come back here, Mum, and do those graves up, now that I'm home.'

'Well, you're the eldest son. It's your job now. I've paid off all the funerals, so there's nothing owing.'

'You're a real old battler, you are, Mum.'

'Ya gotta be!' I replied, smiling at him. 'Can't let anything beat ya—what d'ya reckon?'

We drove out of the cemetery, along the road to Kensington, past the Show Ground, and down Darlinghurst

Road to Woolloomooloo, pulling up outside Pammy's place in Nicholson Street.

Hearing our knock she came to the door and welcomed us inside, planting kisses on our cheeks. Entering the house we could smell the delicious food. She was a deadly cook this Pammy girl, even though she was a vegetarian.

'You came at just the right time. Everything's ready. Come in and sit yourselves down.'

She had the table set up lovely. By this time Nobby was starving as he hadn't eaten since we left Berrima this morning. There was delicious lasagne—vegetable lasagne I mean—and potato salad and a whole heap of tasty things. We got stuck into it, washing it down with cups of hot coffee.

Pam helped Nob get his gear outa the car. We had the rest of the day planned to go and visit as many of the family as we could. Pam waved us goodbye, saying, 'I'll expect ya when I see you, Nobby, after you've seen all your mob.'

We drove away, heading out past the old Rockers pub, then down Wentworth Avenue to Central Station and on to Parramatta Road. First we went to Granville to say g'day to the Allawah Hostel tenants and staff. He'd never seen the place where I was livin. Taking a quick look throughout, he said, 'Mum, ya old robber! Look at all my paintings that you've got.'

'Yes and I bloody well paid you for all of them, and I've got all the receipts to prove it.'

'I can't take a trick, can I?' he chuckled.

'No ya can't with me!' I laughed.

Driving on to see Aileen and Pauline, Nobby said, 'I'm dying for a good feed of Kentucky Fried Chicken, Mum. Ya can't just trot out of Berrima Jail to get a bucket ya know.' He was really hanging out for that damn chicken, and a big grin spread right across his face when I told him there was a Kentucky Fried Chicken joint just near Pauline's.

As we drove into the drive-through, I told Nob, 'Get plenty. You'll have to feed the mob at Pauline's, and those girls of hers can sure put a good feed away.'

When our headlights flashed on Pauline's windows as we pulled into the driveway, they all peered out to see who it was in this big, white, flash car. Seeing it was us, the girls came runnin out and swung around Uncle Nobby's neck nearly pulling him over. 'Ya home! Ya home!' they yelled. Nobby couldn't get over how much his three nieces had grown.

We went inside to feed up on the Colonel's chook, staying for about an hour. Then we headed over to Bidwill where Aileen, the other daughter, lived. Outside Aileen's place we stopped and blew the horn real loud. Next thing, Aileen was at the back gate with a tinny in her hand. She unlocked the gate, and coo-eed real loud when she saw who it was, and called her old man Mick and her two kids to come see brother Nobby. We had more hugging and kissing—I was real proud of the way my kids were with each other.

Oh, don't get me wrong—they had their differences, but blood was thicker than water as far as they were concerned. I'd have to give myself a pat on the back for that, cause I'd always taught them to stick together through thick and thin. We'd been divided and quartered enough in our lifetime in this country that was once upon a time OURS!

Nobby was saying to Aileen, 'You want to chuck that tinny away. It's no bloody good for ya, Sis.'

'Now, don't ya start air-raiding me like Mum does, Bra. It's me only pleasure ya know.'

By this time it was nearly ten o'clock and I said to Nobby 'C'mon, it's getting late, son. Let's go.' So, saying goodbye, we drove back to Allawah where Nob dropped me off before going back to Pammy's. He was picking me up the next day at two o'clock to take me to a lecture I was giving at Parramatta Library.

I wanted him to come along with me to introduce him to the students. Besides, I wanted to show him just what I'd been up to—how to conduct a lecture and handle question time. I knew that I couldn't keep this pace up, with all the lecturing I do, so I needed someone in the family to pass my knowledge on to—and it looked like Nobby was it!

When he arrived at the hostel next day I was all dressed and ready to go. I'd asked Nobby to bring his portfolio of photos of his paintings to show the high school students. Some were doing *Don't Take Your Love to Town* for their HSC. My book was not on the main list of texts that everyone had to read. It was on one of the option lists for English. No wonder we Kooris are on the lowest rung of the social ladder in this country, if our books are not on the main text list.

I'd been told by students that the history books they were set were very outdated European histories, not books that were relevant to our Australian history. But we authors have no say in these things; the Education Department selects the texts.

In the library I glanced around the room and noticed they had a big sign sayin 'Parramatta Library welcomes Ruby Langford Ginibi'.

'Wow!' Nobby chuckled. 'Look at that! My mum's a celebrity.' I poked my tongue out at him. Nobby was happy and talkative before the lecture, but as soon as the students started to come up the stairs and be seated, he seemed to freeze up, startled to be in the limelight with me in front of all these students, he was fairly packin it.

While the co-ordinator was introducing me, Nobby

whispered to me not to pull him into the conversation. Little did he know . . .

'Welcome to you all,' I began. 'I'd like to read my names from the front of my book, to tell you a little bit about myself.' After that I pointed to Nobby, and said, 'This is my son Nobby, who has a starring role in my book.' Nobby was twisting in the chair getting nervous, as all the students' eyes were on him. I did my reading, then threw the session open for question time.

Someone asked: 'In the book, there's no anger or bitterness at the injustices you and your people have had to put up with.'

'Anger is a very negative attitude,' I answered. 'And anger alone doesn't get you anywhere. We are a minority in this country so we haven't got a voice, and besides it was only in 1967 that we were able to vote and be counted in the census. Before that, we were invisible, just like it was right back when Cook arrived and said Australia was *terra nullius*—uninhabited. We have no human rights in this land as long as our people don't have fresh drinking water in some communities and are still dying of curable diseases. And then there's the atrocious rate at which our people are dying in police and prison custody. My son here has done six years in jail for something he never did. The brutal prison system in this country not only has him, but a whole lot of Koori people—women included—in its clutches. The laws we have been forced to live by are whiteman's laws.'

The students started to ask Nobby questions then, and I was amazed because, when he opened up and started to talk, he did quite well. Then he showed them his art work, passing it around the room, explaining, 'If I didn't have my Koori spirit to guide me, I would have been a goner.'

I butted in to say, 'I was terrified of my son going back to jail. The worry that he might kill himself—it was unbearable. You see, if something happens to any member of a family, it affects the whole family. Being incarcerated and locked up away from society, family, and friends, is the ultimate, most de-humanising experience and punishment ever!'

The whole room went deadly silent. You could hear a pin drop.

After the lecture, they all trooped up for me to sign their books. They also rounded up Nobby to sign too, and were all shaking his hand. I glanced at him and could see he was well pleased with all the attention he was getting. Good one, I thought. Now I have one of my mob to pass all my research and educational stuff on to. He's proved he could handle it and very well, I thought.

In the coming weeks I was delighted every time I saw Nobby because he walked around with a perpetual grin on his face—just like that damn Cheshire cat. He was trying to get a job, and also doing some painting, and trying generally to settle into life outside the walls of Berrima Jail.

I badly needed transport, as I was forever doing these lectures and either getting my daughter Pauline to drive me, or taking a taxi to and fro. My adopted son Patrick was the one who changed all that.

Patrick had had a bad accident in late 1985. He'd been hit by a car while crossing the road and the driver had been charged with culpable driving. He'd always been a very active man, been employed, and played football for Redfern All Blacks. But now, poor fellow, he couldn't even move his feet fast enough to get out of the rain. One time we took Patrick to visit Nobby in Berrima Jail, and because he walked with a cane and had a speech impediment, the screws thought he was on drugs and immediately strip-searched Nobby after the visit thinking that Patrick had brought drugs into the jail. Nobby was bloody furious when he found this out. Now ya know why we get paranoid about police. We can't win, can we?

All these years Patrick had circulated among the family: Dianne, then Jeffery, and Aileen, even Pauline. But most of all, Jeffery looked after him, setting him up in his own little flat at Campbelltown so he could keep an eye on him. Patrick had divorced his wife and was missing his little son, Jeffery David (named after my two sons). Jeffery was godfather. But Patrick couldn't look after his son, so he missed out on the visiting rights the court had granted him. He always said he'd make up for everything when he got his settlement.

Patrick had made a claim for compensation with the Aboriginal Legal Service, but four years later had not even collected the police reports or any paperwork to support his case. He asked me to go with him to see if we could hurry the case up. Well to cut a story short, I took him to my solicitors and they took the case on.

Patrick had said, 'I'll give you some money to buy a car, Mum, so Nobby can drive ya around to do those lectures, OK?' He finally received his settlement at this time, and was in the process of buying himself a two-bedroom apartment in Campbelltown so he could get to know his little son again.

Nobby was settlin in at Pammy's; everything was going along smoothly. We'd planned that when we did get that car I'd take Nobby home to meet all his extended family on the mission at Box Ridge, Coraki. I was going to show him all the sacred places to lift him up spiritually. I'd always wanted all my life to bring all my kids and show them my country, but circumstances and no money stopped me from ever doing that.

Each day Nobby was out and about lookin at all the car yards, trying to find a cheap car that would be suitable for us to go home in. We'd planned to go for about three weeks but, because of his parole stipulation, he had to get permission to leave the state. He brought his parole officer

home to Allawah for me to meet her, and she was flabbergasted by Nobby's paintings at the hostel. I also presented
her with my two books so she could get to know all about
Nobby. I thought the books would supply her with more
information than the court papers she had about my son's
so-called 'violent, criminal life'. Perhaps in readin my book
she'd get a more personal view, from our Koori side, of
the situations we are confronted with every day of our lives
in this country.

This was 1993, the Year of the World's Indigenous
People, and I was the first Koori who had been invited to
sit on the panel of twelve judges to judge the 1993 NSW
Premier's Awards for Writing. Wow! Things were sure
lookin up for us Kooris, weren't they?

But I got to wondering why our people had never been
asked into these high social enclaves before. I told the
committee it sounded a bit tokenistic to me, havin me as
a judge in the Year of Indigenous People. They all said in
unison: 'No! No!, We want to right this great wrong. That's
why you're here, Ruby.'

Anyway, I'd come from being at the NSW Ministry of
the Arts all day. When the taxi driver let me out at Allawah,
the girls said: 'You had a visitor today, one of your sons.'
They added: 'There's something on your bed.'

I found an envelope on my bed, with a note said:
'Mum! You knew I was gonna be here today. Where are
ya? Love Patrick.' Attached to the note was a cheque for
eight thousand dollars!

I busted out crying, thinkin, what you give out in life
always comes back to you. This cheque was living proof
of that. I got on the phone straight away to Nobby.

'Guess what was on my bed when I came home today?
A cheque for eight thousand dollars!'

I could hear him coo-eeing at the other end of the
phone.

Next morning he was out here early in the old bomb Holden Premier he'd bought for five hundred dollars when he first came home. It only had two months' registration.

'Com'on Mum, I hope ya ready ta roll!' he said coming into my room. 'I know where there are a few Volvos within our price range.'

'Why Volvo, son?' I asked.

'Well,' he said, 'they're a real well-built car and come highly recommended by Pammy. So let's go—chop chop!'

'Stop hurrying me, I'm not built for speed ya know.' And I hobbled out the door with my quad-stick. We went out to Haberfield to look at this Volvo that sonny-boy had been droolin over for the last two weeks. He told me that he'd been here to check it out several times. I was thinkin the salesman must be fairly sick of the sight of him by now, though I didn't say anything to my big son, aye.

The Volvo was my favourite colour, burnt orange, and the price was five thousand dollars. Nobby told the salesman that the car was mine because the cheque was in my name. Anyway, Nobby would be my driver so that was OK. The money we had left over would be our travelling money.

'We'll be just like toffs, and even have enough to stay in motels when ya get tired of driving,' I told Nobby.

8

YARMBELLAH—GOIN

On Thursday, 22 July 1993, Nobby phoned to say we were leaving on our trip that night. 'I'll pick you up in about an hour's time.' I told him I'd already been packed for a couple of weeks—no problems there. When he saw how much I'd packed, he said 'Ya'd think Mum is going for six months instead of ten days. Look at the gear she's got!'

He hadn't travelled with me since he was about ten years old. Now he was a 38-year-old man, and we were goin on safari together, once again on the road like all those years ago.

Heading on the road to Hornsby on Sydney's north shore, I asked him if he remembered this roadway. He looked at me and said jokingly, 'Trust me Mum, trust me. I wasn't a courier for nothing.' I settled in nicely for the long journey, wishing he'd left it till morning as I was so damn tired.

We seemed to be travelling for such a long time, but I never said anything (like, maybe we were lost) to Nobby.

But eventually Nobby said, 'Seems like it's takin us a long time to get to Hornsby, Mum.'

'Yeah, maybe we took the wrong road, son.'

'We must have.'

We pulled into a garage to ask directions and, sure

enough, we were goin round and around in circles. When we did find our way back to Hornsby Road, I looked at him and said, laughin, 'And you sonny-boy were once a courier, ahem!'

With that he said: 'Mum, shut the fuck up! It's all your fault.' And he was chucklin, having a bloody good laugh.

'Ya know, Mum,' he said, 'It's a damn long time since I've been on *any* bloody road drivin.'

'I can see *that*, son!' I answered, burstin out laughin again.

He was laughin like a lunatic too, 'Shut the fuck up, Mum!'

We passed through Hornsby onto the expressway to Newcastle and I showed him the road to take to Cessnock so we could bypass Newcastle.

'Are ya sure ya know this road, Mum?'

'Yes, me and Pammy came this way when we were going home for research.'

Didn't take long to get to Cessnock, and because it was night time, I mistakenly gave him the wrong directions and we ended up in Maitland and were going around in circles again. We ended up on the road to Muswellbrook so we turned around and headed back to Maitland, then saw a signpost to Raymond Terrace.

'That's the road to take, son,' I called out. 'That's where Jeffery and Shellie used to live. The main road goin north goes through there.'

With that he asked, 'Are ya sure Mum?'

All told, it took us two great travellers six bloody hours to get outa Sydney. I glanced at my son and he must have been thinkin the same thing as me. We nearly busted our guts laughin. He put his foot on the accelerator and we sped on though the dark, cloudless night, still gigglin.

We spent what was left of the night at a motel in Taree.

Then, in the morning, on we drove, through Kempsey, and on to Nambucca Heads and Coffs Harbour.

I told son, 'There's a nice beach here where we can have lunch. It's a good spot. You can jump in the sea to cool off, refresh yourself.' We stopped there for lunch and Nob had a swim and a rest. Then back on the road again heading to Grafton.

Nobby couldn't get over all the banana plantations around the mountains and as far as your eye could see. He said, 'This was the place where, when I was about twelve, the deputy principal of the King's School at Parramatta brought me and Bill.'

I told son that when we reached Grafton we'd be in the beginning of Bundjalung country. It was his country, but he'd never been here before.

'Before white settlement there were 70 dialect clans of the Bundjalung people,' I told him, 'and now there are less than twenty left. Tells you just how much our people and culture were decimated by the so called colonising of our land.'

'Yeah, but no one today wants to take responsibility for that, aye!'

I breathed in the lovely clean, fresh air, and looked at the horses and cattle grazing peacefully in the paddocks as we sped by. I was thinkin I could never get tired of lookin at this country. I was part of this landscape, and this was where I belonged; so did all my kids and grand-children too. It's always been my dream to take them all back there to live, of buying some land and living on it and living from it, and taking care of the land. Having a place called the Melting Pot—there were so many degrees of cast and colour but all in the one family.

We were coming into cane-growin country and I asked Nobby, 'Have you ever seen how sugar grows, son? See all those paddocks filled with all that tall grassy stuff, that's sugar cane. There's acres and acres growing up here. Years ago when I was only a little girl I used to boil the billy for my dad and his cane-cutting gang from Cabbage Tree Island. They worked in the sweating heat of the day, and they were all shiny black from the sweat and the soot from the burnt cane. And there were big old cane punts carryin the cut cane to the big cane mill down the river.'

'It's beautiful country, Mum—peaceful and quiet, not like the city. We gotta move up here.'

I could see that he was getting tired from all the drivin. He was a very fit man—but not superman. We stayed overnight in Woodburn. Next morning we were up and away early. Nobby asked me how far it was to Coraki, where I was born.

I pointed. 'There's the Richmond River across the road, and Coraki is about half an hour's drive from here. But *this* way,' I said, pointing towards the town of Ballina, 'a few miles down this road, is Cabbage Tree Island, where a lot of my mob live too, so where do you want to go first?'

'Let's go to Cabbage Tree first,' he replied.

The roadway through Broadwater and Wardell to Cabbage Tree Island is so close to the river all along this highway; a beautiful place for picnicking or boating. We came to a signpost: ANDERSON CREEK. 'Pull up here, son. This place was named after my grandfather, Sam Anderson the cricketer.'

'So,' Nobby said, 'they *did* name something after great-grandfather after all, even if it's only a creek, aye!'

'Yeah, and now, nearly 40 years after he's been dead I've got historians writing to me for information about his cricketin powers. Shame he never got this kind of attention when he was alive. He was a legend on the North Coast here. They called him the "Bungawalbyn Crack" or the "Prince of Darkness". He scored over 100 centuries in his career but was never asked to represent Australia in cricket because he was a blackfella. They were as racist then as they are now,' I told Nobby, frothin at the mouth.

'Cool down, Mum, cool down. Don't get ya knickers in a knot.'

I looked at Nobby and busted out gigglin. I sure could get fired up real quick about racism against my people.

After a while Nobby said, 'Ya real quiet there, Mum.'

I was thinking about Cabbage Tree Island. It was about 130 acres of flat land. Years ago there was no bridge across the back channel. It was one of the first Aboriginal co-ops—they grew cane, ti tree, and pineapples, and there were several cabbage tree palms, but there's none left now. All the houses were built up on steel frames away from the flood reaches of the old Richmond River that runs into the ocean at Ballina, and the only way on to the island was by boat from the mainland, about 800 yards away. You'd have to stand on the wharf and call out 'Bring the boat over' and wait until they rowed over to get you.

'Thinkin about a long time ago, my son, a long time ago. But here's the turn-off to Cabbo.' And he turned the car left, followed the roadway right around the back, crossing a small footbridge, passing all those cane fields again, knowing that the Island people had some of this cane planted here too.

At the small bridge going over the back channel of the island, I said, 'Turn right. That's Auntie Winny's house, that first one, but let's go to cousin Tubby Bolt's house first. He lives a bit further down.' As we pulled up in front of Tubby's house, Pat, his missus, was on the verandah.

'Where's Tubby?' I called out.

'He's over the other side. That's him fixing that brown station wagon, sis.'

'Thanks,' I called out. We drove back around, pulling up right behind Tubby's car. I held my fingers over my mouth shooshing Nobby as I sneaked up on cus who had his head stuck under the bonnet. I poked him in the ribs and he jumped and turned around.

'Cuso! What are you doing here?'

'I brought my eldest son up home here,' I said, introducing Nobby. 'I want to show him all the sacred places so he can paint and get the spirit of our mob.'

'This is my first cousin,' I told Nob, 'so he's your second cousin.' They shook hands, Tubby saying, 'Gee, he's like ya dad, uncle Henry, cuso.'

I asked Tubby if Nobby could take some photos of him to paint from later while I taped this talk so I could have records for this trip back home. While Nobby took the photos, me and Tubby were into it talkin about our Koori politics. He's been on the Land Council of the Far North Coast for a long, long time. They were workin with the Skill Share, work-for-the-dole program, rebuilding the houses on the island. They were also gonna fix up the graveyard, and make sure all the graves were named and marked properly.

A few houses up the road we pulled into my other cousin's—Doug Anderson—yard. I told Nobby to blow the horn and there was Dougie coming down the high stairway to the car saying, 'Gee Ruby, you're gettin a real rambling rose, aye,' as he cuddled me.

'Yeah, I guess ya could say that, cuso,' I said and introduced Nobby. They shook hands and I asked if Nobby could take photos of him. He agreed and while we yarned Nobby was getting up close taking the pictures. There were some deadly faces here to paint. Then Dougie's missus came down and brought a photo album and gave us several photos to keep, which was real good.

When we were going, Nobby turned the car around to head out when Franky-boy Gomes, who I'd gone to school with on the mission at Coraki, came runnin over to the car soon as he spotted my face. Franky-boy Gomes had married my cousin Judy Anderson. He used to be a park ranger in the Bundjalung National Park and he knew all the sacred sites.

'Can I get a lift with ya over to Box Ridge cus, there's a 21st birthday tonight—one of my nieces?' he asked.

'Jump in then,' Nobby said. 'You can show us the way cross country instead of goin back to Woodburn.'

He sure took us cross country. Boy, was it a bloody rough road! About three quarters of an hour later we were crossing the big new bridge going into Coraki. I remember when I was a kid there used to be a big river ferry across this river, could even carry cars and stock.

The main street of Coraki consisted of about two hotels, a newsagency, a bakery and grocer store and a fruit 'n vegie shop—it was just a village. Anyway it hadn't grown any bigger than when I was a kid. It's funny how things seem so big when you're little, and when you're all grown up you realise they were not that big at all.

Franky-boy was sick. He went into the pub and bought a bottle of beer to suck on.

'That won't make you any better,' Nobby was saying to him. 'It'll only make you sicker.'

'I have to get warmed up for tonight, the birthday party.'

Coming back through the main street after I'd gotten some notepads and pens, we turned right and headed towards the mission. There was a takeaway food place and I got Nobby to get some takeaways, and a couple of loaves of bread and some drinks. I never went over to Auntie's without a feed. I knew they lived in hardship all the time. Nob bought pies, hot chips and cold meats. We passed the hospital, which was called the Campbell Hospital, probably named after one of the first white settlers who were of

Scots descent. They were the 'cedar-getters' who took the land from all our mob—with the Poms too.

As we came closer to the cemetery I told Nobby to turn left. 'The road will take you right to the mission where I was born, sonny-boy.' We were drivin through the gate, and turning right I looked towards Auntie's house and saw it was gone. There was a whole lot of new houses being built. About bloody time, I thought!

'Bloody hell, Mum, so this is where you were born? Look at those old broken-down houses, with paint peelin and the fences fallin down, only for the new houses being built it looks like a Third World country.'

This old mission where I was born was the most ramshackle one I'd seen in all my research up home here. It looked real lonely and sad, like it had no heart, bit like the people here: forgotten and isolated away from the mainstream society with no one willing to help them out.

I wondered where Auntie had gone to now her house was gone. I called out to someone I saw walking by. 'Where's Auntie Eileen?'

'She's in that caravan in that backyard over there,' came the reply.

I got my son to turn and pull up beside the house. I saw her sitting out in the sun in the backyard.

'Hello my Auntie,' I called out, getting outa the car, Nobby and Franky following me. 'This is nunyars jarjum Nobby,' I told her, kissing her cheek. Nobby cuddled her.

'Where's that Auntie Gloria of mine?' he asked her.

'She's inside asleep, she's judung.'

It's sad, but Old Swag, Gloria, had been an alcoholic for many years. She was a trainee nurse before the white husband took her, punched the piss outa her, filled her up with kids, then walked away and left her.

Next thing there were cousins Patsy and Keithy, Old Swag's sister and brother, coming out the door to meet us.

111

'How ya goin, cus?' they asked.

'Hello,' I answered, kissing them both and introducing Nobby. 'These are Auntie's jarjums, son, Patsy and Keithy.'

They shook hands and welcomed him saying 'Old Swaggy always talkin about you. She calls you "big chalk".' They all cracked up laughin. 'That's her with all her nick-naming people.'

Auntie told them to make some tea. 'Gajalgahny Patsy.'

'I bought some pies, chips and boodengh [bread] for nungingh [food], Auntie,' I told her, asking Nobby to get the food out of the station wagon.

We all sat under the shade of the trees. I spotted tita Gert over the road and called out to her, 'Tita, come and meet nunyars jarjum [my child]. You haven't seen him since he was a little jarjum.'

'I'll be over in a minute,' she called back.

'Gee,' Nobby said, 'I haven't seen Auntie Gert since I was about twelve or thirteen, aye Mum.'

'Long time ago, son.'

Gert came across the road sayin, 'Gingo, you gettin a regular visitor up here, tita.'

'Yeah, you know who this fella is?'

'This not Nobby, aye?'

'Yeah,' I said and Nobby grabbed her, cuddling her saying, 'Hello short stuff, that's what Mum and Auntie Neridah used to call you.'

Gert asked what we were doing up this way. I told her that I brought Nobby up home to meet all his extended family and show him all the sacred places. I told her that he was the only one of my jarjums that has even been home where I was born.

Aunt Eileen replied, 'I would have showed you all the special places in Bundjalung National Park. But I can't go with you cause my eyesight is goin on me. The older ones won't hand down the knowledge of culture to the young ones here because they live in such hopelessness and they don't want to know. They've fallen prey to all the social ills that come from white man's way of livin. They're too busy drinkin themselves stupid. There's no elder men to kick em up the arse and make em get out and live properly and strive and work. Once my family were stockmen and women. Nowdays, people have nothin. No pride, no hope.'

Just after lunch we said our goodbyes and drove outa the Box Ridge mission. As we drove along, I could see Nob thinkin.

'Mum, I didn't know that some of our people were still living in such poverty! It really knocked me in the guts. Just bein in jail, even though it was terrible, it was a hundred per cent better than that place where you were born.'

'That's what I keep bumpin my gums about son, trying to educate people with my talks, about conditions on these places. Nobody gives a damn! If those bureaucrats in Canberra that control all the funding were to come and see this, maybe they'd understand but they don't get off their bloody arses to even come to these communities to have a look for themselves. They have the Kooris that work for the government and they are too busy lookin after themselves to bloody care about anyone but themselves. There I go again. Frothin at the mouth.'

'Settle down Mum, settle down,' Nobby said, laughin at me.

About 500 yards down the road from the mission was the Coraki Cemetery. We had to turn left to go down the back of the cemetery to one of the remnants of the racist colonial past. The whites were up the front, and we were right down the back, fenced off from the rest.

'Pull up here, son. This is where our people are buried, and I want to show you grandfather Sam Anderson's grave.'

And we climbed through the fence to the biggest grave there and it was grandfather's. The good people of Coraki buried him here and provided a headstone. It said 'Two grand cricketers—Alex James and Sam Anderson.'

'Whata ya reckon, son?'

Nob was standin in awe lookin at it. 'So Mum, this is part of our history that we'll never find in white text books. This is my great grandfather, aye, who stumped Sir Donald Bradman out for a duck.'

'Yeah, son, you should know there was only two Aboriginal cricketers ever to get Sir Donald out for a duck in Australian history. One was your grandfather Sam Anderson, and the other was Eddie Gilbert from Cherbourg Mission in Queensland.'

Nob stared in silence.

'Have a look around now son. This is our segregated section of the cemetery. When I was a kid here there were segregated picture shows. Roped off we were. Blacks on one side and whites on the other. Segregated hospitals— one ward down the back with "Abos only" on it. We weren't allowed into mainstream schools. We only had our little Mission school where we were taught by an untrained teacher. There was even a racist crow in the baker's shop where we went to get some bread every coupla days. Soon as we'd step in the door the crow, who had a silver chain around its leg and sat up on the counter, would call out "Mum, there's blackfellas in the shop." Fancy *him* callin *us* black. We'd a liked to get him and wring is bloody neck cause nobody would be blacker than him.'

Nob and I walked outa there chucklin. Then we headed out on the road to Nimbin where I wanted to show Nobby the Nimbin Rocks. Travelling along Nobby and me were takin in the scenery.

'This is bloody beautiful, Mum.'

'Yeah, you wait till ya spot the Nimbin Rocks, you'll freak right out! They're so spiritual.'

There were a lot of twists and turns before we got to the outskirts of Nimbin. At the next turn in the road I called out: 'Look son, there's the Rocks. Can ya see them?' There they were, the three big spirals of rock, jutting up to the sky.

Then we travelled the rest of the way into the main street of Nimbin. I told son that years ago it was a thriving hippy community. I told him all about the Rainbow Cafe, and the people who were sick of the fast life in the city who'd come lookin for spirituality. They thought that Nimbin was the place, being a very sacred place to Kooris from here. It thrived for a while then all the drugs and rejects landed, and the place is still surviving on being a tourist place. They sell everything on the street stalls: jewellery, craft, clothes and prohibited substances. I'd heard by the grapevine and the newspapers that there were some huge drug busts and even some drug murders here so the place had some character.

We parked in the street. A lot of people were shopping. It was a Saturday and cars and bus loads of tourists were roamin all over the place checking the stalls. Nobby spotted a cassette stall and moseyed over while I headed for the nearest loo. He came back to the station wagon real excited. 'Mum, I got Rodriguez and some good Elvis ones you'll like, even a Jose Feliciano—ya remember him?'

He bought some cool drinks and sandwiches, then we headed out of town towards the rocks. One local had told him where he could get up real close to take his photographs. He turned right onto this dusty road, and all the while he was driving he was stopping now and again to get glimpses of those very sacred rocks.

Soon we were up real close. We both got out of the car to get a good look. There was a great silence between us. We gazed in awe at this sacred place and I told my son the legends about the Nimbin Rocks.

'These rock formations were pushed up through the earth's crust in the great volcanic era millions of years ago. This was the sacred home of Nimbunjie, the warrior who guards the master's teaching place. It's not a woman's place. It was the place where the clevermen, we-un-gali, were taught to throw their spirits and levitate. They got their great powers there. They had the power to heal and the power to kill. It's so sacred that when they went there they called out to Nimbunjie to let him know and when they went they picked a branch off a tree and even brushed their footprints off the ground where they had trod to leave it undisturbed; that's how sacred it was. Even today, people who go to climb there have seen this spirit warrior. He comes to them in their sleep with his spear and the people who desecrate his teaching place have bad nightmares.'

I looked at my son after telling him all this and he said, 'I can feel the power even here and we are only on the roadside. Mum, it's real powerful—and eerie. I don't think I'd like to sleep around here at night.'

After he took the pictures we left that sacred place. To show respect for Nimbunjie I called out in lingo, 'We gonna yarmbellah now nuguthung'—we goin now grandfather—and we drove away sadly. We had not desecrated Nimbunjie's dreaming place.

We stayed overnight in Lismore, and were up and breakfasted before eight o'clock. We headed out of town going back over the bridge towards Coraki. On the other side of Coraki, as we sped along the road, I pointed out places of great memories to me. Lismore is situated in a valley. Nice town, with some lovely streets and twenty minutes' run to beaches on the coast. It was 26 kilometres to Coraki, all properties of ti tree, grown for oil, and heaps of bamboo trees, guava trees, wild cherries, and lilli pilli.

'There son, this part of the river was where me and another bigger girl nearly got washed down the river in a boat. I was about seven then. This bigger girl told Dad that she could row a boat and we were sent to ask the people across the other side of the river for some matches to light a fire to cook the fish Dad'd caught. When we got into the middle of the river the current was running too swiftly; this girl never had the strength to turn the boat and we were bein washed downstream with Dad shouting out which way to row. Lucky for us the current took us back into the bank or we might have been goners, aye!'

It wasn't long before we were driving across the little bridge into Woodburn.

'You want to go for a run around Evans Heads?' I asked Nob. 'Come on, I know Bundjalung National Park, and I want to have a swim in the salt water like I did when I was a kid!' I also wanted to see the 'sit down place' and the Gammagarra—the sacred scarred trees.

I told Nob, 'There are eight of these sacred scarred trees and they represent eight of our tribal elders who were murdered by drunken whites.' I needed to show all this to my son—he was gonna be the one I handed all my knowledge of culture to. This was what our people were doing long before the white man came to our land.

[All but two of these trees were subsequently cut down by developers, despite the protests of Laurence Wilson, the Bundjalung elder who is the keeper of that place. Laurence Wilson eventually went to court and got the construction work stopped because the developer had put the road in a different place to what was approved by the Richmond River Council. But that doesn't bring back the trees. They're gone forever. Now the Richmond River Council is re-zoning Crown lands so that Bundjalung People cannot claim it through Native Title.]

So the two of us headed out for Evans Heads. The heat

was so intense, and as we sped along the wind cooled our faces. Soon we were crossing the bridge, then going up around the point, and taking the side road that led us to a little beach. Then we were outa the car, with Nobby running for the water, and me hurrying as fast as I could to sit my bum in the water. Son was diving in and out of the waves while I clung to the shore line. I had my big Bombay shorts on under my kaftan dress, and I just lay down, enjoying the cool water. I went further out and all of a sudden a big wave knocked me arse over and I could hear Nobby laughin at me while I spat out the salt water I'd swallowed. Nobby was singing out, 'Hey Mum, I didn't think anything could knock *you* down!' I headed back to the shore and sat on some rocks to have a spell. I pointed out a kite bird flying, as an F111 shot straight out from Goanna Headland, though we couldn't hear it for the roar of the sea and the waves splashing on the shore.

We only stayed a little while, then we drove slowly through the Bundjalung National Park. I showed Nob where there was Koori land up on the headland: it was called Dirawong Reserve, Goanna Headland. The legend of the creation of the headland is that a snake began tormenting a bird, and Nimbunjie, that Bundjalung man with extraordinary powers, called out to the goanna to come and protect the bird. The goanna chased the snake from Bungawalbin across to where Woodburn is now, and eventually found it near Evans Heads. The goanna was slowed when the snake bit it on the head and, when it caught up again, the snake headed out to sea and then doubled back to the Evans River and lay down, thus creating Snake Island. The goanna reached the sea and lay down to wait for the snake to return. That's how Goanna Headland was created.

We drove on silently through the Bundjalung National Park. I was amazed that it hadn't been destroyed by bushfires. But it had been badly burned further down towards Grafton and Yamba. I glanced at my son and I knew the magic of this special place would have a profound effect on him.

We pulled up right on the bank of the Evans River, overlooking Snake Island. Nobby and I got out of the car and sat on a big log watching tourists out in the river fishing and joyriding in boats. The noise shattered the peace and serenity of this very special place.

'Mum,' Nob said, 'this place is real magical. I can feel the spirits here. It's so tranquil, except for the motor boats.'

'Yes, I can sense that too.'

I sat wandering back in my thoughts to the times when the Bundjalung tribes, my people, fished and swam and cooked their food here—the fishes they had caught. And in my mind I could hear the crackle of the fires. I could even smell the fish cooking. Even hear the lingo spoken, just like it was only yesterday. We stayed an hour or so, and I was just spellbound by the beauty of this tribal place.

In 1842 a big massacre of a lot of my people happened here. I remember the old ones saying: 'Go to the Bundjalung National Park and enjoy picnics and barbecues but don't camp or go to sleep there, because our spirit ones will walk around you with their spears and frighten the hell outa you.'

I said to Nob, 'Come on. Let's go. It's getting late.' So we left that magical place with my son still awestruck about feeling the spirits of our ancestors there all round us.

Tell me about Bundjalung National Park and your feeling on seeing it.

It's a place where I'd like to spend the rest of my life,' Nobby said, 'but that will have to wait. The noise, the bird calls, rosellas, and lorikeets screechin, the peaceful presence of this very spiritual place had me spellbound. It's God's country, Bundjalung country, and it's a concern to me the way people treat the land. Anyway, I loved it up there. I'd like to retire up there one day and live there for the rest of my life.

9

WE BELONG HERE

Next morning, we headed towards Ballina, then up the coast to Bangalow—up in the big mountain ranges before Byron. All around us were mountainside farms of macadamia orchards, acres and acres of them, with avocado trees too. Years ago I remembered these hills around Bangalow were littered with banana plantations, nearly as many as Coffs Harbour and Nambucca Heads. There were paw paw plantations too, and over the years the banana and paw paws disappeared and were replaced by the macadamia and avocado orchards. Here, high up on this mountain range, we could see all around, even the ocean at Byron Bay. Nobby was spellbound. Sonny wanted to get some avocados to take with us in the esky. We pulled into a roadside stall and he came back with about three dozen avocados. I had a knife in my bag and we tucked into some straight away. Nobby was sure makin up for all the good tucker he couldn't get in jail.

We drove through Byron Bay, Murwillumbah, then inland towards another special place—Mount Warning. I told son that the tribal name for Mount Warning is Wollumbin.

'Captain Cook called it Mount Warning because it's the highest point on the coast here and would warn the ships that there were reefs out in the water. In tribal ways, Wollumbin means "cloud catcher" or "weather-marker". Lovely names aye, those tribal ones.'

We could see outlines of Wollumbin in the distance and the closer we came to it the more it had Nobby fascinated. He kept stopping the wagon while the light was good enough to take photographs.

'This is not a woman's place,' I told Nobby. 'Only initiated men can climb this mountain. Before the white man came, this area was known as the "big scrub". Then the cedar-getters came, so it's not the big scrub now. All the great cedar trees have gone, but there's still plenty of bush turkeys.'

We drove on again and were soon bypassing the Gold Coast. Son's eyes were fairly poppin out of his head with all the pretty women wandering around. Oh, he was a typical male with eyes for pretty girls, aye! With all these new highways it made me think Queensland sure was going ahead with this tourist business; there were tour buses goin everywhere. We passed Sea World, then the Magic Kingdom, also Movie World. America was movin in fast too; wasn't only the Japanese who practically owned this state, but they had old Joh Bjelke organising that a long time ago. Now Australians were screaming, 'Too bloody many overseas interests in Australia. They are takin all the wealth out of our land . . .' How ironic they said they were takin all the wealth out of our land—'Our land?' This is the land that they stole from all the Aboriginal people of Australia. Even today, 1998, with the Mabo and Wik legislation, we Kooris are still fighting the pastoralists and miners over this land!

We arrived at my sister Rita's place in Brisbane about tea time. Turning into Rita's driveway I looked up and saw the curtains opening and spotted my niece Janna. Next thing she and Rita came down the long stairway to meet us.

After dinner, Rita bedded me and Nobby down. Next morning, we headed out, with Rita driving ahead of us giving us directions on how to get to Kilcoy where my cousin Shirley (Midge) lived. Driving along the road you could see the Glasshouse Mountains, a whole heap of them sticking up in the sky. Nobby was flabbergasted by them, and pulled up to take more photos.

As we sped along the highway, I remembered back to the times of this big son's imprisonment. I can't begin to explain the sheer joy—the pleasure—of being able to sit and sneak sideways glances a him to check that it was him *really there* in the car driving with me. Doing this also brought back the memories of his father and of how much he looked like him now he was all grown up and outa that damn jail.

But I sure wasn't gonna tell him that cause he'd be spewing. As far as my kids were concerned, they only had one parent and that was me, though I do remember telling them, 'Look I didn't make youse all by myself; ya know it takes two to tango!'

'Yeah but you raised us and battled for us all our lives. Where the fuck was our father, aye?' Nobby said. 'He was never ever around for us kids as we were growin up. You're the only role model we kids had, Mum.'

Well what could ya say to that, so I just shut up my mouth. Besides, it wasn't worth arguing about. What they said was very true. Where the fuck *were* their fathers? I often wondered. They were well and truly there for the making of these kids but not for the responsibility of rearing them. But then, their loss was my gain, aye. As compensation for this, each Father's Day I received cards from all my kids, so I was the lucky one. What do ya reckon?

On the outskirts of Kilcoy, with its beautiful hilly countryside, there were acres and acres of pineapples growin everywhere, and large pine forests, even a big abattoir for slaughtering cattle and sheep.

Driving into the township I directed Nobby to the park and showed him the Yowie, but since I was last here, in 1985, someone had desecrated his private parts—cause he had none! The Yowie was a giant hairy man creature who was supposed to live in the caves and mountain areas of the Great Divide. He was seen many times around the Tooloom scrub years ago, and this statue in Kilcoy Park was about eight feet high and made of cement.

At the end of this street was the home where my cousin Midge and her husband Dougie-boy lived, right on the side of a hill. We turned into the driveway and climbed the hill, pulling up outside the back fence. There was Midge and Doug coming to meet us followed by their yapping little chihuahua dog.

'How long you gonna stay?' Midge asked me.

'Just today and tomorrow,' I said, introducing Nobby. 'This is your Uncle Doug and Aunt Shirley, but I've always called her Midge.' They hugged. Doug and Midgie had been married for about 45 years. Dougie used to ask me when I was gonna get hooked up again. I'd answer, 'When I can find someone just like you,' and he'd crack up laughin. I sometimes envied the loving, long-lasting marriage that they had but, alas, it wasn't meant for me to have the same lifestyle.

Dougie helped Nobby bring the bags in from the car while Midge made a pot of tea. We yarned and reminisced about the old times in Bonalbo where we were raised. Midge showed Nobby where he was gonna sleep downstairs. They had a self-contained flat underneath the house and it had two big bedrooms and a lounge, kitchen and dining room too. Nobby said, 'Gee, it's a big house Auntie Midge.'

'Yeah, but we're only renting it.'

After we settled down, Midge started to get tea ready and shooed me away when I offered to help. 'You must be worn out with all the travelling you and your big son are doing. Go sit down.' And I did like she said cause I was real tired.

Next morning we were up early and getting dressed for our trip to the Glasshouse Mountains where Nobby wanted to take pictures to paint from. Up front with Nobby was Dougie-boy with his ten-gallon hat and dark glasses. He'd had his eyes operated on for glaucoma. As we drove out onto the highway Nobby told Uncle Dougie he'd have to direct him. 'Yeah, I'll do the best I can,' he replied. He was nearly blind but he still knew the way.

Midge and me were sitting up in the back like queens, with our eyes looking at the countryside as we sped along. We headed towards Maleny. We could see these huge mountains jutting straight up to the sky just like they were pushed up through the earth's crust, which they were. We were on the Bruce Highway and heading to Nambour and, before we knew it, were at the Big Pineapple and decided to go in and have lunch. Nobby was amazed by the place. You could go into the pineapple and climb right up the top, and go for rides in the little train that takes you all over the plantation. There were macadamia trees, bananas, mangoes, and pineapples growing. It had restaurants where you could have meals, buy all the tourist stuff: jewellery, postcards, craftworks, everything.

After a long time on prison rations, Nob couldn't get over all the exotic foods here—ice creams, and banana splits with macadamia nuts. He'd never tasted macadamia nuts, so when I bought him a large packet that were freshly roasted, he was still munching on them when we finally found the road into the Glasshouse Mountains.

There was a viewing area with tourists getting photographs from this high place. The view from here was real deadly.

I got to rememberin the legends of these mountains. Tibrogargan, the father, and Beerwah, the mother, had many children. Coonowrin (the eldest), Beerburrum, the Tunbudla twins, Coochin, Ngungun, Timmeroowuccum, Mikeeteebumulgrai and Elimbah. According to the story, there was also Round who was small and fat, and Wild Horse (presumably Saddle Back mountain), who was always straying away to paddle in the sea.

One day, when Tibrogargan was gazing out to sea, he noticed a great rising of the waters. Hurrying off to gather his younger children in order to flee to the safety of the mountains to the westward, he called out to Coonowrin to help his mother, who was again with child, escape the floods. Looking back to see how Coonowrin was assisting Beerwah, Tibrogargan was greatly angered to see him running off alone. He pursued Coonowrin and, raising his club, struck him such a mighty blow that it dislocated Coonowrin's neck and he has never been able to straighten it since. When the floods subsided and the family returned to the plains, the other children teased Coonowrin about his crooked neck. Feeling ashamed, Coonowrin went to Tibrogargan and asked for forgiveness. Filled with shame at his son's cowardice, Tibrogargan could do nothing but weep copious tears which trickled along the ground and formed a stream which flowed into the sea. Then Coonowrin went to his brothers and sisters but they also wept at the shame of their brother's cowardice. The lamentations of Coonowrin's parents and his brothers and sisters at his disgrace explain the presence today of the numerous small streams in the area. Tibrogargan then called Coonowrin and asked him why he had deserted Beerwah. Coonowrin replied that as Beerwah was the biggest of them all, she should be able to take care of herself. He did not know that Beerwah was pregnant and that this was the reason for her great size. Then Tibrogargan turned his back on Coonowrin and vowed he would never look at him again. Even today, Tibrogargan gazes far out to the sea and never looks at Coonowrin who hangs his head and cries, his tears running off to the sea. His mother, Beerwah, is still heavy with child. (It takes a long time to give birth to a mountain.)

Remembering this legend, I knew that I had a few Coonowrins of my damn own. With that thought I fixed my gaze on my son. He was just like Coonowrin, always runnin away to play in the water and always getting into trouble for it!

After a good night's rest back at Midge's place, my big son was up early before breakfast packin the bloody car. When Dougie said, 'You're an early riser boy!' Nobby replied, 'They don't let ya sleep-in in jail, Uncle Doug. They kick ya in the guts and say "Come on, get up. This isn't a bloody holiday camp." That's the sort of treatment we got. But I'm free now, aye!'

'Musta been bloody hard in there,' Doug answered.

'Ya had to be strong to survive. Lucky I've got plenty of Mum's fightin black spirit in me,' Nob said, smiling at his uncle.

When Midgie and Doug came out to see us off, my eyes got misty. I hate sayin goodbye to people I loved.

'Ya know Mum, those are REAL PEOPLE,' said Nob as we drove away. 'They're the ones that make life worth livin, aye.'

'You're so right, son.'

'How come Mum, ya never told us kids anything about

Uncle Doug and Auntie Midge before, or where they lived?'

'I did tell you lot all about the people from up home, but you were real little then. That's why you don't remember them. Besides, Doug and Midge moved to Kilcoy and most of their kids were born there,' I said.

We planned on driving to Esk, then Ipswich, and onto the Mount Lindesay Highway over the border back into New South Wales, then to Woodenbong, and Urbenville. Crossing the countryside, we headed towards the little township of Boonah. This is where my grandfather Sam Anderson was born, at Purga Mission, near Devon Creek around 1880.

As we travelled, I told Nobby some more about Grandfather's cricketing powers. In the 1913-14 season at Casino, he scored 1038 runs (including five centuries) at an average of 148.3 runs. At another time, 1919-20, his highest score for a season came at Lismore. He scored 1458 runs with nine centuries at an average of 121.5, including his career highest score of 261 not out.[1] So we had Aboriginal achievers way back then, not that they were given much recognition, and it's still the same today.

'How about them apples, son?'

'It's really inspiring, Mum.'

We'd just passed Mount Barney. There were several other mountains—big rocky outcrops, some large ones and some wide ones. They were volcanic mountains, very beautiful to gaze upon.

We were on the Mount Lindesay Highway, heading towards Woodenbong and, as we got closer, the outline of Mount Lindesay itself—Julbootherlgoom, sacred home of the hairy men spirit—came into view. Nobby was stunned by its size. 'Holy cow, it's huge,' he yelled.

The legend of Julbootherlgoom says that it was once a tree, which a man climbed with a vine in search of honey, cutting footholds with his stone axe. During the night, the tree grew into a mountain and the footholds can still be seen today on the side of the mountain. The oral tradition also tells of a whiteman who came to the area of Woodenbong, Unumgar and Maroon. He climbed Julbootherlgoom and when he reached the top, he met an Aboriginal man. The two came to blows, and both men fell over the cliff locked in each other's arms. As a result the Kooris stayed away from that area for a long time. Today, people living in the area have noticed that when the sun strikes the western cliff face of Julbootherlgoom at a particular angle, a very clear figure of an Aboriginal man is visible in the shadow formations.[2]

Nobby was fascinated when we got up real close to Julbootherlgoom, comin through the twists and turns of the mountain road. I got him to pull up and listen to the sounds of his country talkin to him. As he got out of the station wagon, the sounds of the bellbirds and an occasional whip bird, makin its whip-crackin sound, could be heard. We were both spellbound. Just across the road, straight opposite us, was the foot of Julbootherlgoom. I sat in the car while Nobby walked across the road and into the canopy of the tall timber reaching for the sun with flecks of sunlight peeping through, giving it a magical effect: the peace and serenity of this beautiful forest, the great Tooloom scrub, with the sounds of the birds calling out just like they were saying, 'Welcome back to your land and your Dreaming.'

When he came back to me Nobby said, 'Oh Mum, this place is so spiritual to me, more spiritual than Uluru.'

'It should be son, it's your country,' I answered. Then we drove off and left that magical place.

As we were coming into Woodenbong I told my son that this place was where I used to go and collect mushrooms just after the rain—me and Iris McBride, with his sister Pearl and brother Bill when they were little.

We drove on to Urbenville and then through another rainforest called Yabbra, with more bellbirds calling 'tinkle tinkle'—like little bells they sounded. Not far away was Tooloom Falls, Dirrangun's territory, our cranky old witch-woman of the 'before creation period'. I could hear her call loud and clear, echoing through the tall timber and creeping vines.

'Hey son, I'll tell you the legend of Dirrangun because this is where I got your tribal name from—Bulagan. It means "hero, handsome young man" in Bundjalung language. The legend says that Dirrangun was a cranky old witch-woman who was always nasty. She was from the before creation period. Years ago we could never use her name. It was *jung* or bad to say it out loud, though now the legends are being told it's OK to speak it. She lived up in the big scrub known as Tooloom, and she was very jealous of her son-in-law, Bulagan. Because she didn't like him she hid the drinking water by sitting on the spring. When she wasn't there, she covered it with vines and leaves so no one could touch her water. All the tribe went looking for water because they were very thirsty but she was so nasty that she kept it hidden. One day the water came up out of the spring and she held it back with her body. The force of the water was so great that she had to move her right leg and the Clarence River was formed as the water flowed out. The water was getting harder to control and hold back so she moved her left leg and the Richmond River flowed from under that leg. Pretty soon the force of the water carried her out to sea screaming because she was so nasty. The Clarence and Richmond Rivers run into the sea at Ballina and Yamba. Another version of this story says that Dirrangun didn't get carried out to sea but is still there in the Clarence River, at Grafton, in the form of a big old tree trunk in the water. Another version again says she is there in the rocks on the beach at Broadwater and even at Ballina.'

'I like that name Bulagan, Mum. It suits me,' he said with a chuckle. Soon we were on the other side of the Yabbra Forrest.

I pointed out Mount Haystack to Nobby, sayin, 'Ya wanta hear a real deadly traditional story about that big flat top mountain over there, son?'

'Yeah, Mum, ya gotta teach me all these things, aye?'

Nooloigah belonged to the place now called Yabbra Forest. He was a good hunter and fighter and because of this, he was an elder who knew the law.

'One summer day, Nooloigah took his youngest wife, Bani, to hunt for possum (black buck ganam). Nooloigah climbed a tree where some possums were sleeping but one woke up and ran down the tree. The ganam ran right over Bani's feet and off into the scrub. Bani chased the possum but she got a surprise when she found it dead at the foot of the trees.

'Now it happened that Nooloigah's younger brother had also gone hunting and when he saw the possum running towards him, he killed it with his killing stick (murundan). Hearing a noise, he stepped back and hid behind a tree. Just then, Bani came running up. Bani bent down to pick the possum up. When she looked up, she saw her brother-in-law standing there. He looked very handsome in his red-ochre warrior's paint (gudjin). Bani felt very attracted to her brother-in-law. She came close to him and took him in her arms. They pressed close together until the young man was overcome with shame and ran off towards the camp. Meanwhile, Nooloigah was thinkin that his wife had been gone too long. Just when he was getting angry, Bani came up with the dead possum in her hands. Nooloigah wondered how she could have killed it because she had no murundan. When Bani handed the ganam to him, Nooloigah noticed that she had gudjin smeared on her body. Nooloigah didn't say anything, but he was sad because he knew his wife had been with another man.

'Back at the camp, the aunt of Nooloigah put the possum on the coals to roast. Nooloigah walked over to the batchelor's camp (djanangan). It was there he thought he'd find his wife's lover.

'Under a possum rug, Nooloigah's younger brother lay asleep, shivering as if he were sick. "What's wrong, brother?" asked Nooloigah.

'"My head is aching," his brother answered.

'Nooloigah went back to the camp fire and brought a cooked possum back to his brother. "Eat the fat of this possum and you will feel better." As he sat up to take the possum, his cloak slipped down showing that the younger brother was covered in smudged gudjin.

'So, thought Nooloigah, My own brother has stolen my wife!

'Now in those times the penalty for wife-stealing was death, but the punishment had to be given by the elders. Nooloigah knew this but was overcome with anger, and he rushed at his brother with his charmed spear (bilar). After a terrible fight, Nooloigah killed his own brother.

'The elders felt that Nooloigah should be punished for taking the law into his own hands. A clever-man (wuy-an-gali) began to sing a song that made Nooloigah very sick. Nooloigah dreamed his brother's spirit came to him and asked, "Why did you kill me, brother? It was Bani who did wrong." The words of his brother's spirit echoed through his mind until Nooloigah felt his own spirit weaken. Nooloigah cried out, "I have murdered my brother, I have murdered my brother!" The sounds echoed through the forest, haunting all the men (baygal). Then Nooloigah, too, passed into the spirit world. But because he was such a great warrior, his body did not disappear. It became a great flat-topped mountain. The whiteman (dagay) called this mountain Mount Haystack, but its Aboriginal name is Nooloigah. Some say you can hear Nooloigah singing on windy nights. Others say it's only the wind (Nyar).

'This legend was told to me, son, by Auntie Charlotte Page who was related to my mother and Auntie Bertha Stuart of the Gidabal People of the Bundjalung tribes.'

Nobby said, 'Oh, what a deadly traditional story, Mum. Look, I've got goose bumps all over me.'

'Yes, it's beautiful,' I added as we travelled on. 'I have to hand all this traditional knowledge on to all you kids of mine. Then you can educate your kids so our culture will survive,' I said.

Soon we were near the old Bonalbo Homestead, eight miles away from the town of Bonalbo. I showed Nobby the cemetery where all the Hinetts were buried. Bonalbo residents were going to commemorate the graves. Thomas Hinett was the head stockman of Bonalbo Homestead. He was Midge's grandfather and the house we were raised in was the old outer station house, given to the Hinetts by the owners of Bonalbo Station for years of service to them. I told Nobby that this town was where me and my two sisters Gwen and Rita were raised by my father's brother, Sam Anderson, and his wife, Auntie Nell. It was in the 1940s when we lived here.

When we rounded the mountain coming into Bonalbo, I pointed out the showground, and the hospital where his sister Pearl was born in 1952. Nobby wanted to take photos, so we drove up there to the hospital.

'I used to work in that laundry there and wave to your big brother Bill and sister Pearl over in the school yard just on the opposite hill. And in the ward where I was when Pearl was born, the possums would come through

the window at night and steal my fruit. And the nurses
that nursed me were my school mates and it was so hot
they carried Pearl around on a pillow with only a nappy
on.' Nobby was chucklin, imagining from my words what
I was rememberin.

'Ya know, Mum, I can still remember how much of a
chatterbox sister Pearl was, aye?'

'Yep,' I answered.

Down from the hospital we turned left and I pointed
out the school, and also the church yard next to it where
I'd jumped the fence chasing a Vigaro ball and landed on
a broken bottle, cutting my foot real deep. Then we drove
down past Stewart's bakery where Midge worked a long
time ago. Bonalbo was a little town nestled in a valley. It
was surrounded by hills. The industry here was a Norco
butter-making factory, cattle sales and a huge timber mill
where my father carted logs from the Tooloom scrub. There
was a bank, pub, a post office, two garages, a chemist, a
stock food shop and one cafe. That was Bonalbo!

Later I showed Nob where the old house we were all
raised in used to be. After driving round for a while I took
him to the pub where I'd worked as a chamber maid and
helped the cook out on cattle sale days when I was only
about twelve or thirteen. This town was full of memories
for me, although a lot had changed since I was a child. As
we drove out of town, we saw a signpost stating that
Bonalbo's population was 500. This was a lot less than
when I lived there as a young girl.

We travelled on for about fifteen minutes before we
were on the Bruxners Highway. To the left was the road
to Mallanganee and Casino, but we turned the car to the
right, heading towards Tabulam.

'I like the look of this country, Mum,' he said, 'It's so
peaceful.'

'Yes, son, this place we are goin to is my mum's

country, Tabulam. The tribal name for it is Jabulm. It means "we belong here" in Bundjalung language.'

'There's some beautiful tribal names, aye?'

'Yeah, but the whiteman didn't recognise them. Renaming the country with his own names was part of taking possession of it.'

'Is this the Great Dividing Range we are going towards, Mum?'

'Yes,' I answered, 'we'll be climbing that range after we get to Tabulam . . .'

'I've never seen country like this before, Mum. The air's so fresh and clean,' Nobby added.

Soon we were coming into the township of Tabulam. We asked directions to the mission and travelled on to the outskirts of the town. I wanted to see Auntie Mary and Uncle Mick Walker, my mum's first cousins, about a tape of the Bundjalung lingo that Uncle Mick was doin for me. I kissed Auntie Mary's cheeks, introducing Nobby sayin, 'This is nunyars jarjum, Auntie.' She kissed Nobby, and told me that Uncle Mick, her brother, was away in Casino teachin the lingo. 'Will you give him this note and nagam [money], so he can do a tape for me of the lingo?'

'Yes, I'll do that,' she answered, then we said our goodbyes and left, as it was late.

I noticed that this new mission had solar heat on top of the homes and they were beautiful homes too. 'You see, son,' I said to Nobby, 'this old mission we gonna drive through, it's called Gunningah-nullinghe, which means listen to the voice of the people.'

'You're an authority on the language yourself, Mum,' said Nob.

'Yeah, well I find out all this through the research I do. I didn't always know. The break-up of our family unit meant that I didn't have access to all this knowledge. I've had to struggle to pick it up from anywhere I can.'

Turning left on the road we were going to climb the Great Dividing Range and go on to Tenterfield. As we climbed up higher, it was quite windy. There we were—us two travellers goin on safari—with our dark glasses and Akubra hats with our land rights colours—red, black, and yellow—flying in the wind, catching the sun's glint. The air on this Great Dividing Range as we climbed higher and higher was real crisp and clear. I could smell pine and eucalypts. Some farms were burning timber too. In some of the valleys there was a smoky haze and rosellas screeched as they flew by.

'You wanta have a drive, Mum?'

'OK,' I said, jumping at the chance to have a go. I'd not been behind the wheel of a car for a bloody long time. So Nob pulled over to the side of the road and with pounding heart I turned the key, gunned the motor, and took off, travelling at a safe speed on this rugged mountain road that seemed to go on winding forever.

My startled son said, 'Ya doin real good, Mar. I never thought you could drive at all.'

I drove for about ten miles then decided the roads were too winding for me, so I let Nobby take over again.

Driving into Tenterfield, we looked for the bottleshop where my school mate, Ray Hannan, worked. I went to school with him in Bonalbo when we were kids. After we tracked him down, I introduced Nobby, and he took us back to his place, telling us, 'Make y'selves comfortable while I go pick Peg up at work.' (His wife, Peggy, was a nurse.) So me and Nobby had the house to ourselves.

They arrived home and it was like old home week with all the rememberin and reminiscing about our childhood days. They also wanted a look at Nobby's art too.

Next morning we were up and had breakfast and were on the road by eight o'clock. I gazed out at this beautiful countryside and told Nobby, 'I loved these mountains and valleys, also the peace and contentment of this place. It always played a big part in my life, and it seems to keep drawing me back here, time after time. The cattle and horses grazing and swishing their tails to keep the flies off. Such tranquility! And peace. This is our real belongin place, son. We are connected to this land, me and you, and all our family.'

'I can't get over this country,' Nob replied. 'I realise I've never been this way ever before, and for you to be taking me and showing me all these places in Bundjalung country, it's bloody wonderful, Mum.'

We journeyed on, the music from son's tape keeping me wide awake because he was playin it too loud as usual—Yothu Yindi singing 'Treaty now! Treaty yeah!' The next place we were passing through was Glen Innes, then on to Armidale. It was a big place with lots of colleges and churches.

Coming through the little town of Uralla, Nobby suddenly gunned the motor and sped outa there real quick.

'What are ya doin, son?'

'Well, Mum, that's the bloody place where the gungies chased me when I was comin back from Auntie Rita's in Brisbane when I was havin a breakdown. Remember?'

'Well, ya don't want to go speedin, because they might be here waiting for ya again!' With that we both busted out laughing.

At Tamworth we fuelled up again, and drove on, heading for my sister Gwen's place in Gunnedah where we were gonna stay the night.

'You haven't been up this way either, son, have you?'

'No, Mum. The only place I was at was Tamworth in the boys' home when I was a teenager, remember?'

'Yeah, I remember.'

'In that place we used to have to scrub the floors on our hands and knees; had to run everywhere we had to go; never allowed to walk; never allowed to talk except when we were spoken to by the staff. Tamworth Juvenile Correctional Centre was the equivalent of Grafton Jail, the toughest jail in New South Wales.'

'So these places still have bad memories for you, son?'

'Afraid so. I think they'll haunt me for the rest of my life.'

Some idiot mates of mine, Wayne Towney and others, we stole a car and in the boot of the car was a big briefcase full of brand new Citizen watches. So it didn't take long for the coppers to grab us, like all of us little blackfellas with brand new watches on walking around Redfern, showin off and bitchin up to our mates, givin em to family and everybody. We ended up gettin pinched for stealin a car and watches and goin to Albion Street shelter where, if you're over sixteen, you're on remand like Yasmar. I got sentenced to twelve months' boys' home because I'd already escaped from Gosford boys' home. I was sent to the hardest boys' home in the whole of Australia, Tamworth Boys' Home. It was run by a mongrel of a governor called Braden, and at our first sight of each other me, I hated him, and he hated me.

Tamworth was an old jail, and they turned it into a boys' home for the worst offenders in the system, so it was just like Grafton Jail, but for boys. Before we came to Tamworth Boys' Home, me and two mates of mine did our week at Grafton Jail (the Big House) and this place was where all the absolute crazies in the system existed in the one jail, and it was not legal for us boys to be there, but they jumped around with the paperwork, and Christ knows what, and anyway I ended up in Tamworth Boys' Home. It was a total shit fight for about five months while I was there. They had a ladder system where if you were good, did everything right, polished your shoes, and sucked up to the screws you climbed the ladder, and once you

*are on top of the ladder you were close to goin back to Gosford,
a minimum boys' home.*

*One night I was lucky; something came over my head, and
this person said, 'Now keep ya mouth shut, or your gonna stay
here, if ya open ya mouth you won't go back to Gosford Boys'
Home.' So I kept my mouth shut, went down the stairs with
this hood over my head. That was how they escorted you outa
the jail at night time—put you on a train and you ended up
at Gosford Station at nine in the morning, and that's when
they came and picked you up and you ended up back in
Gosford.*

*I was there for nearly three weeks and being an ex-
Tamworth Boy all the screws have got a lot of respect for you
because you've gone to the Big House, they thought it was the
discipline. You were like a fuckin robot when you came back,
clicking the heels like a grenadier guard. I was back at Gosford
for about three weeks, and this bloke 'snotted' one of my little
mates—he bashed the shit out of my little mate so I squared
up with him. And I was on muster and this bloke was pushin
me in the back, wanted to go on with it, so I turned and went
'smack!', and it was subsequently adverse points against me for
fighting. So they locked me in the boob for 24 hours and I lost
a lot of points. I came back to work when I got out and the
old feet got itchy again. They said 'quick march' and I just took
off. I was out again, but that's what Tamworth Boys' Home
and Mount Penang Gosford was like.*

Our next stop was Coonabarabran where we lived in a tent
when Nobby was a kid a long time ago. About seven miles
out I saw where the old Burrabedee mission used to be.
Pointing it out to Nobby, I said, 'That mission was seven
miles out—long way to walk into town to get a feed if you
ran outa tucka.'

'Yeah, you'd be starvin before you got the food.'

'I think the old mission managers only took the mission people into town one day a week to shop.'

It was just coming onto late afternoon as we drove into Coonabarabran. We decided it was enough travelling for the day, and we booked into a motel for the night. The next day, we went to have a good look around the old place we'd lived in a long time ago. We drove around the town, and I noticed the changes. I asked Nobby if he remembered anything about this place. He was a baby when we came here.

'Not much, Mum. Only the way to the school, back that way,' he said, pointing. 'I must have been about eight years old when we lived here, aye?'

'Yes, I think so,' I replied.

Then we were goin on the road we came in on last night back to the Gunnedah Hill, where Mum Ruby Leslie and her daughter Brenda lived, and Neridah Chatfield, my old mate who I christened 'Neddy'. She lived on the hill too, or so I was told.

Rounding the corner of Gunnedah Hill, we drove up and parked the car in front of the house I thought Brenda and Mum Ruby lived in. Mum Ruby Leslie was one of the Stolen Generation. She was put into the Cootamundra Girls' Home and then sent out into domestic service when she was a young woman. She eventually found her brother and sister again, and she was able to make her way back to her home country.

There were about five houses on this little mission. Now, as we pulled up, there was Brenda coming to meet us saying, 'Gee sis, good to see you!' She cuddled and kissed me and Nobby too. 'Come in and have a cuppa,' she said, leading us into the back of the house.

'Let Nobby go in first,' she said, 'cause Mum's there. See if she remembers him.'

So Nobby went into the house first, and the old girl

was sitting in a big chair. Soon as she saw him, the old hands went out to him. 'Nobby my boy, what are you doin here? Where's ya mother?'

Nobby gave her a kiss and cuddled her sayin, 'Here's Mum, Nan.'

She turned her dear old face to see me and smiled up big, sayin, 'Ruby, good to see you. You come to stay awhile with me?'

'No Mum, we're just passing through. Me and Nobby just called in to see you before we go back to Sydney.'

I asked Brenda where Neridah Pearl was, and she answered, 'I'll go and sing out to her'—which she did, callin, 'Neridah, there's someone here wants to see you.'

There was a fence about three feet high between the houses, so I pulled up a seat under the tree, and sat near the fence callin out, 'Neddy Pearl Chatfield, where are ya?'

Next thing she was there standing on her verandah, with a walkin cane. She started to cry soon as she saw me, and she called out to her grand-children to get another chair for her to sit and talk with me at the fence.

When she came to sit on the chair, I could tell she was tiddly—been charging on with her kids. There was Danny her son, Cynthia her daughter, and Cindy Lou and Warwick, her grandchildren. They all came out to the fence to see me and say hello.

And me and Neddy Pearl reminisced about old times, and all the battling and hardship we'd shared. We laughed at both of us being members of the walkin wounded, as we both walked with a walking stick. I was overjoyed to see her, and I said, 'Sing to me, tita,' and she started singing, 'You Don't Have to Say You Love Me', and 'The Green Green Grass of Home'. The tears were rolling down her face as she sang. I got up quickly sayin, 'I've gotta go now, tita,' the tears welling up in my eyes too, and as I rounded the corner of the house I busted out cryin. Nobby

141

was there to comfort me and I told him, 'I don't want her to see me cryin. She's still drinkin and killin herself with the booze.' It hurt like hell to see tita like that.

Then Nobby wanted to see where our old bush camp was. This house was where I carried the water from, seven days a week, when I had my two tents pitched over the back in the fifties, a long time ago. I asked Brenda to take Nobby and show him the place where the camp was.

'You comin, Mum?' he asked.

'No, I'll wait on the roadway for youse. I can't go there. Too much hurt for me to face up to.'

They were gone for a while, then when they came back, Nobby was real excited.

'Gee Mum,' he said, 'the three small pine trees ya had for our toilet, with the hessian bag all around it, and an umbrella on a branch in case it rained—they're still there! Only now they're real big full grown trees. And I could hear all the dogs barkin, even hear in my mind's eye brother Dave sayin, "Ha ha, ya can't catch me Nobby. Ha, ha!" And brother Bill callin out, "Big nake Mum, big nake!"'

When he told me all this, tears welled up in my eyes with the rememberin.

'Come on,' Brenda said. 'Leave the past behind, sister. Leave it behind.' And we walked back with Nobby's arms around the both of us old girls, comforting us.

10

ART AND THE JUDGE

I went up to Brisbane for Warana's Writers' Festival in September 1993, and for a while after that I didn't see much of Nobby. He was busy trying to sort his life out. He'd moved into a little, one-room, self-contained flat in Glebe as things had not worked out as expected with Pam at Woolloomooloo. Well, he was a person that liked to do his own thing.

It's difficult for folks on the outside to really understand what being locked up does to people. After doing time in custody, it's not easy to cope with being suddenly set free. There's a period of adjusting to life on the outside, and it takes time to come down from all the built-up hype of coming out into the world again. It did present Nobby with some social and psychological problems. All our family had to give him space, to let him adjust at his own pace to life outside the prison walls. I was amazed at how well adjusted he was. Must've been my attitude—rolling with the punches that life gives us—rubbin off on him, aye.

'Tell me what it's like from your point of view about bein out of jail?' I asked Nobby.

It takes a long time to adjust from jail to civilian life because it's a whole different kettle of fish. Outside, if someone tells you to get fucked, you just brush it off and walk away, but inside you pull out knives, iron bars, and fuckin go for it, no beg pardons. In jail, it's who's in first wins. It's a big shock to you when you first come out of the jail system, just about everything scares the shit out ya, and every time a cop car goes past ya, you fuckin run around the corner and hide, and even though you're a free man, you still think that they're after you. Just adjusting to travelling on a train, even riding on one scares the shit out of ya, or a bus, the only safe way to get around is by taxi, but not havin much money and bein fresh outa jail, you can't afford many taxis. It takes a long time to adjust.

He took me to look at his little room in Glebe. It had all the conveniences in it—sink, tap, stove, and fridge, a wardrobe, single bed, a table and two chairs. I thought it wasn't big enough, but he was used to being cramped into small spaces. He had his twelve-foot easel set up near the window, and all his paints packed neatly in empty plastic milk containers beside it. I marvelled at how tidy and organised he was. He kept a neat room, but then he was always a workaholic, a tidy man, even when he was a kid.

I remembered back to Green Valley, and my Housing Commission home in the early seventies, when I'd say to him, 'I'll give you a race to clean up this place. You start in the bedrooms sweeping with the broom, and I'll do the washing-up and clean the kitchen.'

'OK. You're on, Mum!' he'd say, grabbing the broom, and pretty soon the dust'd be flyin. (We had no floor covering in those days.) I just took my time with the washing-up, and he'd poke his head around the corner sayin, 'Mum! You still ain't finished yet? You conned me again!' And he'd be laughin and so was I. But when all the kids were little, I'd taught them that everyone had to pull their weight; that was the only way we could survive. And that lesson came in good stead now.

He agreed, now he had the station wagon, that he'd run me to all my lecture appointments. This worked out well as I was able to ask for petrol money to cover travel expenses, and Nob was only on the dole, which only paid for the room and some tucker. We started off with a Volvo, then it was too expensive. Next was a BMW!

It was a whole new world of communication, the lectures and talks about Koori art and culture, and I dragged him into every discussion I had. I drummed it into him: 'We are the first people of this land, yet we get no recognition of having put anything into the settling of this land. They have glossed right over our history, and I want you to learn all this from me, so you can pass it on to the next generation, and anyone who wants to have knowledge of our people and our land. I want you to stand up, and be proud of who you are! The jail is behind you now. No more! Gone! Finished! You've given nineteen years of your life to the jails and brutal correctional places in New South Wales. You've had to go through all this trauma to find your true Koori spirit. I'm the only black connection you have to your culture, because your father's white. So throw off the chains of oppression, and live through your art! That's what you were meant to do. This is your Dreaming. The jailing you've done let you discover your true Koori spirit. And you damn well *have*, son, for all those years you've been hitting back and fighting against the racist jailing of our people. You are not, and never have been, alone. Your story is that of every other Koori who's been jailed and in trouble with whiteman's law. So go forward; don't look back! Because I'm so proud that you've found your true spirit, and that you've survived. Me and you and our whole family are survivors in this land.'

When I'd tell him this, his eyes would light up, and he'd get the biggest grin on his face, like all his worries had been lifted from his shoulders. He'd say, 'I'm planning to paint the history of our people through what you've taught me, Mum. It will be documented so the whole world can see what it was like for our people up in Bundjalung country and that the knowledge is invaluable. I'll never tell anybody what you've told me Mum, but I'll hand it on through my paintings.'

I was doin a lot of lectures and talks—too many—but I couldn't seem to say no when people asked me. It was too important for me to educate people whenever I could. Nobby often took his portfolio of photos of his art and showed them to the students I talked to. It was a way of promoting his work. One day I had another lecture at Wollongong University. Nobby drove me down there, and we had lunch with the teachers, then I lectured to about 150 students. I introduced Nobby before my talk, and afterwards they crowded around him looking at his portfolio. He sure was lapping up all this attention. But afterwards, when he took me back to the hostel I was feelin woozy, and a few days after, I had a bad cold and ended up in hospital with the worst bout of bronchial asthma I ever had. I was very run down.

I told Nobby and my other kids that I wasn't gonna do any more lecturing. I was literally killin myself tryin to educate people about us Kooris. I said, 'I've done enough. I'm not gonna bust my gut any more tryin to edu-ma-cate them.' (Famous last words, aye!)

But after a while I was bustin to get out and about. I was bored stiff from restin, restin—boy, was I was rested! So on 12 December I had a day out with Nobby and my grandkids, Jaymi and Davey-boy. We were going to the cemetery, then to the Botany Inaugural Aboriginal Arts Awards, at the Airport Central Hotel, to see some of Nob's paintings, then on to the Writers' Centre at Rozelle where I was doing a reading.

Since the death of my son David, his children Jaymi and Davey-boy had been raised by my daughter-in-law, Debbie. Nob and Debbie hadn't spoken for the nine years since David's death. He'd blamed her cause she'd run away and left David. But now I was glad Nobby had forgiven Debbie. The old wounds had healed over the years, and Nobby wanted to get close to his dead brother's children, to somehow make amends and feel connected to David through his children. When they got into the car, I could tell he was having a great time tormenting the two of them, messing Jaymi's deadly hair-do, and wrestling and slapping Davey-boy around each chance he got.

But the closer we got to the cemetery, the quieter we all became. Davey had never been here to see where his father was laid to rest, but I'd brought Jaymi out once just last year. Now Davey and Jaymi bought some flowers at the shop, then, as we drove through the gates, I was thinkin I sure know this road well: I've buried so many of my family here.

Nobby pulled the car up at Dad's and Pearl's grave. We got out and I said to Nobby, 'You take them up to David's grave, son. I'll sit here and talk to Dad and Pearl.' So he headed off with the kids up the hill about 40 yards away to where my two sons were buried. I pulled weeds off the grave, and talked to my daddy and my darling daughter Pearl, telling them how much we missed them, and asking Dad to look after my jarjums.

Before long, Nobby came back down the hill, leaving the two kids alone so they could share their grief for their dad. They came back down about twenty minutes later and Davey was crying uncontrollably. Then I heard the sound of my totem bird, Willy wagtail, calling out loudly, 'Kitchee! Kee! Kitchee, Kee.' I grabbed Davey and cuddled him sayin, 'Hear that Willy wagtail bird, Davey-boy? He's my totem, and he's callin out to let ya know that ya dad was pleased you came to visit him, you and your sister.' With that we drove out of that very peaceful place, overlooking Botany Bay, but the two kids were real quiet until we were well away from the cemetery.

Wasn't long before we were in Mascot and turning into the Airport Central Hotel where the art exhibition was. We went up two floors in the lift, then entered this big, cool space with the most deadly Koori paintings all around the walls. I got the kids to drag a chair for me so I could move around and look. There were only two art attendants there; one knew Nobby, cause he'd been back and forth like a bloody blue-arse fly, delivering his paintings. For this inaugural Botany Aboriginal Art Awards he'd submitted the paintings he'd done of me, Max Silva, and Pam Johnston. I thought they were real deadly. He didn't win, but his paintings stood out well. I was real proud of him and, as he said, the showing was good promotion for his work.

Max Silva was our black magic man of music, a drummer, and singer of the Black Lace Koori band, who had taught my son Billy to play the drums in the late sixties. Max had died of a heart attack, so Nobby, out of respect, painted Max's spirit: with his little cap perched on his head, looking down smiling on Everleigh Street, Redfern, it was deadly.

The painting Nobby did of me was painted from a photo, same as Max's, in Berrima Jail. It was a portraiture of me with my first book, *Don't Take Your Love to Town*, with the Koori spirits rising from the earth to the skies. And Pam Johnston's portrait was of Pam looking at our old elder Auntie Eileen Morgan. The painting showed Auntie's old home on the Box Ridge mission with Pam's long dreadlocks hanging down, and again the Koori spirits rising from the earth up to the skies. Real deadly they were.

One of the ladies visiting the exhibition came up to me and said, 'Your face is very familiar to me.'

'That's Ruby Langford Ginibi,' Nobby butted in, and the lady said, 'Oh! I read your book, and loved it. Wait till I tell them at home that I met you!'

I said, pointing at Nobby, 'If you've read the book, you'll know about my son Nobby. He has some paintings in this exhibition.'

Turning the attention onto him made him blush and say, 'Come on Mum; time to go.'

But the lady had already grabbed his hand and started shaking it, saying, 'Gee! I've actually met someone I read about in a book, and also the author.' Nobby was blushing again as he led us to the lift, with Jaymi and Davey-boy chucklin at their uncle's embarrassment.

We drove up O'Riordan Street and over to Glebe Point Road, where Nobby pointed out Glebe House. It was the place where David had died.

We dropped in to see Nobby's little flat in Bridge Road, then headed off to the reading and Christmas party at the Writers' Centre. It was at the old Rozelle Psychiatric Centre, and as we pulled in there the kids and Nobby joked about how if we didn't conduct ourselves properly, they might not let us outa there! We went inside and I wished they had air conditioning; it was so hot and at every little exertion I was puffed out. Oh well! I was whingeing all the time about the heat, but I'd worn my red dress so they'd see me comin, nar! My stars told me it was my passion colour; besides you never know ya luck in the big city, aye!

There were about 50 or 60 women there and a few men. I read 'Shame Day: My Birthday' from *Real Deadly*, then we all settled down to some eating and drinking. No alcohol was the order of the day. Faith Bandler came and sat next to me yarning and I showed her my two books. Lookin at the photographs in *Read Deadly*, she was flabbergasted because she realised she knew my mother. I said,

'My grandmother, Mum's mother, came from over your way, Tweed Heads, Billynudgel.'

Then another woman in a straw hat came over and said, 'I loved your story "Shame Day". I'll have to buy your books.'

Faith introduced her, saying, 'This is Justice Elizabeth Evatt, Ruby.'

I nearly fell over, but managed to say, 'I'm glad you enjoyed my story. Here, you're on the Law Reform Committee, you can have my two books with my compliments.' As she thanked me, Nobby winked at me.

Driving home, I thanked my big son for making it a special day with the kids. 'You know, Mum,' he said, 'I'm your taxi driver now.' He dropped the kids off, then me, then off he went back to his little room in Glebe. He was tired too, I could tell. But it had been a proud day for us both.

The next week, the staff and residents of Allawah decided to hold a Christmas barbeque and party. Nobby said he'd cook—as long as I gave him one of the six Christmas puddings I'd made. Everyone chucked in, and all the staff and the families of the residents brought food, so we had plenty to go around. The girls on the staff at Allawah helped me make the punch. I'd made two lots, and they were called 'the good punch' for the children—and 'the bad punch'—the one with alcohol.

There were about 30 people there counting the children, and it was a bloody good day. We had Christmas music, and even some old favourites from the sixties. My daughter Pauline showed up with Kevin Bloody Wilson's tape of 'Living Next Door to Alan', and 'Santa, Where's Me Fuck'n Bike?'. It was what is called a bawdy tape. 'Pauline,' I yelled, 'put that bloody filthy tape off! Those old girls are listenin you know!'

She changed the tape real quick to Christmas carols,

but then I remembered the old girls were deaf so they couldn't hear them anyway. When I told Pauline this, the others busted out laughing, saying, 'Ya mad Ruby, ya mad!'

With all the time he'd spent behind bars, Nobby hadn't been around for many Christmases with the family. This was his first Christmas with us in six years. So it was a very special occasion, and a damn good time was had by all.

But just a few weeks later, trouble came again for Nobby.

On 22 January 1994, I got a phone call from a constable at Annandale Police Station telling me he had Nobby in custody. As he was speaking I could hear Nobby swearing and cursing in the background. Oh my God! I was thinkin, here we go again.

The policeman asked if I'd like to talk to him to calm him down, but I could hear Nobby yelling out, 'Don't come here, Mum! I don't want ya to see me like this! They've bashed me!' The policeman wanted me to come along and bail him out and take him home. So the bottom fell out of my basket again. I told the copper I'd be right down. I rang Pauline and I started to cry as I was telling her what had happened. She picked me up and we went down to the police station. When we got there I told them I was Nobby Langford's mother, and they asked me to be seated. We waited and waited, but nothing happened and no one told us anything more. Then I was called into a side room by a young policeman and told that Nobby wasn't there but had been taken to Prince Alfred Hospital after he'd tried to hang himself with his jeans.

'Why didn't you tell me this before?' I demanded. 'I've been waiting out there for three-quarters of an hour.'

I was so furious! The total disrespect of some policemen is so unbelievable, unless you've witnessed it, or it's happened to you personally.

He asked me if Nobby was suicidal. I replied, 'If he was suicidal, why hasn't he suicided over the last nineteen years of being incarcerated in Her Majesty's Prisons?' The police officer didn't know what to say.

I went back out, sat down with Pauline, and we waited a further half hour. Then I was called into the sergeant's office and told that Nobby would be back soon and I could take him home as he was only charged with a misdemeanour. I told the sergeant who I was, and said I was writing the story of my son's life, about the years he had given to the prison system. I told him my son was a respected Aboriginal artist, and that I'd been researching Aboriginal deaths in custody. I told him it was a big shame on Australia that the killing times are still with us. The police sergeant said it was procedure to take prisoners to hospital to have them checked out. The police sergeant couldn't give a damn. I could see it annoyed him to even try to explain to me (a black woman) what was happening to my son.

When I went back out to the front office, Pauline said that Nobby was here in a station wagon out front. She went out to see him but came runnin back in tears, cryin, 'Quick, Mum! Come and talk to im! He's kickin and swearin at em. Come quick!'

I hurried out to the station wagon, startin to cry myself, and pleading, 'Come on, son. Please behave. Now we gonna take ya home. The sergeant said it's only a misdemeanour. Stop goin on now!'

Lookin at him made my heart bleed as he was hand-cuffed with only a hospital smock and a pair of jockettes on. They'd taken away his jeans, and I screamed out, 'Where's his clothes? He's a human being y'know!' Nobby was spittin and kickin at the police as they manhandled him out of the station wagon. His eyes were wild like a terrified, lost animal.

Inside the police station he calmed down enough for them to formally charge him. He had one false tooth, and I noticed it was missing; his eye was very black, and he had cuts and other bruising, but he was basically OK. Pauline angrily asked the police, 'Where did he get the black eye? He couldn't do that to himself!' I told them I was going to lodge an official complaint.

When Nobby finally got into the car with us to go home he was still hyped up. 'Rotten bastards,' he said. 'They reckon I smashed a car window but I didn't do that at all, Mum!' We took him back to Glebe but he wouldn't let us come into his flat, sayin he just wanted to have a good sleep and settle down. Pauline took him to his door, and I could see him cuddlin and kissin her goodbye. We drove away, hoping he would be OK.

Next day he rang to tell me what had happened.

A mate showed up after I got home to Glebe. We went around the corner pub for a couple of shandies, then his sheila showed up and joined us. She was commin on to me, and me mate, he's Koori too, put something in my drink (bombed it). He king hit me from behind, so I came up swingin. We ended up fightin outside the pub and we fell up against a chinaman's car, nearly broke the window. Someone called the cops, the Koori bloke stole my wallet and ran off! By that time the bombed drink had wiped me right out. That's how I ended up in Annandale cop shop.

I didn't know what the bloody hell I was doin cause of what me mate put in my drink. It was a trip I was told later. It's supposed to spin ya out, ya see coloured lights and I don't touch that shit. I snapped out of it at the police station and the police alleged that I'd tried to put a noose around my head and hang myself with the belt of my jeans, whatever, and I think that's one of the reasons they let me go out on self-bail. I think they were scared shitless that I was gonna do something *stupid. Anyway, I didn't know it then that it wasn't the police who'd bashed me. I had cuts and a black eye. I had more bark off me than a gum tree. I thought that the coppers had kicked the shit out of me, but I was told after by one of my neighbours that it was one of me great mates that got into me. And it's the first time in my life that I ever went back to a police station requesting the days that these officers would be on duty, and I stood in front of four coppers and apologised to them, even though I didn't like doin it. In a strange way it made me feel good. I was fined $75 for language and given a suspended sentence of six months.*

It was kinda funny if you could see the humor in it, but I didn't feel like bloody laughin. Because of all the police violence and racist treatment of Koori people in the past, me and Pauline were thinkin it was the coppers who had bashed Nobby.

'Pick decent friends next time,' I told him, to which he answered, 'Never again, Mum, never again.'

'Famous fuckin last words, aye!' I said.

The whole the time he was recuperating from this drama he was paranoid about his broken parole, worrying that it might put him back behind bars. He was fairly shittin himself. I tried to cheer him up sayin, 'It coulda been worse, son.' Even after all that'd happened to Nob, I was still shaken by how easy it was for my son to attract trouble. I knew he never went lookin for it; life's dramas always had a way of hookin up with him and throwin him around, givin him a good shakin up every time.

But now something else was about to shake him up—in a different way! Nobby met a girl in the pub where he used to play pool in Glebe. Her name was Megan, but she liked to be called Megs, and they became inseparable. It was good to see Nob in a steady relationship. I kept thinkin, I wish he'd settle down and get married. Can't be a

bachelor all his life and play the field. On weekends they'd
come to visit me here at Allawah, bringing my favourite
Red Rooster chicken with potato wedges. We'd sit on my
bed munchin out and yarning about everything.

Next thing Nobby was asked by Russell Bruce of the
Aboriginal Enterprise Centre to get a collection of his art
together for an exhibition at the Bondi Pavilion. Through
the Department of Social Security he got a room at the
Randwick Community Centre to use as a studio. Nob was
so excited about his first solo exhibition, and he set about
getting organised to do the paintings. He had three months
to get 40 paintings done.

First thing though, we got rid of the BMW; it was
costing us too much in upkeep. So much for my son's
expensive taste in cars. We swapped the BMW for a
Commodore sedan. What a comedown! From Volvo, to
BMW, to Commodore. But the Commodore worked better
than the other two.

A few times me and Megs went over to Randwick
together to see how Nobby was doin with the art work.
He complained constantly about too many interruptions.
You can just imagine the amount of noise there was each
day at the Community Centre, it was not like the quietness
of jail.

*I was renting a studio at Randwick Community Centre, and
because there was so many distractions throughout the day, like
old people's dance classes, day care lunches, community meetings, there was just too much noise, and I had 40 paintings to
hang at Bondi, so I decided to turn into a bat and paint at
night time. I used to get there at six o'clock at night and the
lady that runs the joint gave me a set of keys so I could let
myself in and out.*

*This got me thinking about workin in jail. I started out
bein a 'waits yard sweeper' which means you clean the waits*

yard, keep everything in order, see if everything is put back in its right place. I was made the 'activities yard sweeper' with a very good friend of mine, Jason. And I was the activity sweeper for God! two and a half to three years, agh, that meant I was trusted. I had to go out to Bowral, accompanied by an officer. We bought all the inmates' runners, shoes, sox, or, if they wanted, electric jugs or TVs, anything they could buy up. I used to go out and get them, and towards the end of my sentence, when I was more than trusted, I was a 'C3'. It's an outside warrant. You're unsupervised. It's the best security you can get, that C3 classification. The officer would leave me at one end of the street and say, 'I'll see you in about three hours.'

When Nobby took to painting at night time, that worked out better for him, but he forgot to eat properly because of getting so involved in his painting. So he lost about a stone. I roused on him sayin, 'You want to damn well pull up and bloody eat a good meal ya know, or you'll collapse before ya finish son!'

'Yeah Mum, I'll have to pack sandwiches, or go get takeaways. I'm gettin too skinny, aye?'

He was also running out of canvases—can't buy much out of the dole after paying the rent on his little room in Glebe. So the family chucked in and we bought him some canvas to help out.

The exhibition was to be held at Bondi Pavilion on 19 July 1994. Time was running away on Nobby. He only had 28 paintings done. So he called on friends who had bought his artwork while he was in Berrima Jail. He called on other friends and family too, then he had enough for the exhibition.

The works were looking real good. I was very proud of him, especially since he'd asked me to name some of the paintings for him. He wanted tribal names, so here are some of the names I used: 'Moogim' (Perch), 'Julm' (Fish),

'Bunihny' (Porcupine), 'Bingingh' (Turtle), 'Jambang-Janbang' (Platypus Dreaming), 'Dirrawong' (Old Man Sand Goanna), and 'Gulumbi' (Wallaby Hunt). Megs documented them and made the fliers advertising the exhibition. Then the invitations were sent out, and we were all gettin excited as the time drew near.

On the day of the opening, Megs did the shopping for the food. Me, Anna Robertson, a friend of mine, and Megs' mum Margaret, got together to do all the catering at Anna's place in Bondi on the morning of the exhibition. Nobby and his mate, Macka, finished the hanging and checked that everything was OK. Then we all lobbed up at the pavillion at about six o'clock for the opening. Pauline and my grand-daughters helped arrange the tables and food, the booze was packed in ice, and the drink waiters arrived right on time. Real posh, I was thinkin.

When I first entered the room and saw all Nobby's paintings around the walls, I stopped dead in my tracks. I'd never seen some of the finished works done by my big panicky son over these last three hectic months. Ah, it was so damned stunning. My son had done wonderfully well. It was beautiful, so beautiful. All the hassles and dramas of his life, and he could produce this outstanding Koori art. I nearly choked because there was a big lump in my throat. Nobby had the painting he did of me with my book, and many of the others I knew, and there was a coffee table Nobby had a mate make for him on which he painted the whole theme of the exhibition; it showed a mother crocodile and baby one, and was titled 'A New Beginning', it was beautiful, such intricate work. I was spellbound.

Nobby came over and asked, 'Well, what do ya think Mum?'

I grabbed him and cuddled him, sayin, 'My boy, you've outdone yourself. This is fabulous! I'm so damned proud of you. You have really found your Dreamin, son.' I started to get misty eyed, and he said, 'Don't start cryin Mum, or you'll bugger me up too.' Then we busted out gigglin, and he led me to a big comfortable chair he'd set up in a good spot.

People started to come in then, and Nobby hurried away to welcome them. I looked across at him and thought, he looks like he's handling it well. He was dressed in his black jeans, black shirt, and black boots, with a red tie and an Akubra hat with the red, black, and yellow band on it.

As the time came to kick off the exhibition, the place was filling up with people. Nobby had asked his sister Pauline to act as Mistress of Ceremonies. About 6.45 pm I asked Pauline to start things rollin, so she picked up the mike and introduced the Warrabri dancers.

Dave Whitton, their boss, introduced each dancer. There were three young boys, the littlest being about five. When the littlest boy danced alone, the clapping and whistling was tremendous. Dave spoke about how important it was to 'teach our children the dances and the songs, and about our culture, so we can keep the traditions alive.' Then the didgeridoo's gutteral sound flooded the whole room, and away the dancers went—sh, shh, sh, with the sound of the clap sticks keeping time, clack, clack, clack. Everyone's eyes were on the young dancers, all painted up in ochre, with red jarby-jarbys on. The next dance was the Shakey-leg, and the last one was the Cheeky Kangaroo. Sh, sh, sh, they went, mesmerising everyone with the sound of the didgeridoo. The dance had everyone entranced. The spirits of our forefathers were sure here with us mob on this night.

A big round of applause followed when they finished their dance. We'd hired a video fella to film it all, so we'd always have a record of it. Pauline then introduced me to launch the exhibition. She handed me the mike and I said:

'I'm very proud and honoured to launch my son, Nobby Langford Balugan's first exhibition ever.

'He took up art a few years back. It was a means of survival and helped him keep his sanity. And as you can see by his paintings, he has really found his Dreaming. His art speaks for itself.

'For those of you who don't know much about Aboriginal history, culture, and or politics, I will say this to you: our ancient, timeless Aboriginal history began many thousands of years before Captain James Cook graced our shores. Some Aboriginal people are called "contemporary artists", but in fact they are a continuation of the traditional ones.

'When you see dots on Aboriginal paintings, it represents grains of sand. Traditional art was done in the sand. Our people did their sacred ceremonies, then the sand was kicked over, so no one could see the sacred design. To do the paintings, they broke a twig off a tree branch, then chewed and masticated it at one end until it was soft and pliable. Then they dipped it in the many colours of ochres, then they painted on bark and cave walls. It was not until 1972 that Aboriginal people had access to acrylic paints. We adapted. We are great adapters. We Kooris have *had* to be, because we have always had to conform to the standards of the invaders of our country.

'I am an elder of the Bundjalung people of northern New South Wales and south-east Queensland. Because my son wanted a tribal name, I call him "Balugan", after the son-in-law of our cranky old witch-woman of the before creation period. Her name was Dirringan. "Balugan" means "hero", or "handsome young man". My son likes that!

'I'll finish with this poem I wrote, called 'Singing the Land'.

Our ancient tribal people sat down
and sang the spirits into this land,

giving it its physical form.
Whiteman called our Dreamtime a myth;
our people know it as a fact.
It was before 'creation times',
they sang the mountains, valleys, rivers, and streams,
they sang life in all its vastness into this brown land.
Never has it been silenced by whiteman
or his destructive ways.
And the song had a beginning
and there will never be an ending
until justice is returned to the singers of the songs, our
ancient tribal people! And us urban Kooris too!

'I'd now like to declare this exhibition—titled "A New Beginning"—open. Thank you.'

Then I called out in my lingo, 'Balugan nunyars jarjum! [Handsome young man my child] Welcome back to your Dreaming!'

Then Nobby came across the room and cuddled me, with the people still applauding. It was a magical moment for me, and the tears were misting my eyes. I don't know how he ever survived jail, but then I knew he had the good spirits of our Koori dreaming, and our family's dead ones, watching over him too. This was a turning point in his life.

Pauline took the mike back and said, 'I'd now like to introduce my big brother, Nobby Langford Balugan, the creator of these wonderful works.' Much applause. Then Nobby took the mike off Pauline with one hand, and wrapped his free hand around her neck so she couldn't get away; and they stood there, brother and sister, with everyone lookin on.

The nervousness showed in Nobby's face, and he said, 'I'm not used to talkin into a mike.' He was looking at the mike moving it around nervously in his hand. Pauline had to grab his hand and hold it still. Then he went on, 'It's quite an experience for me, so all I can say is thanks for commin. I'd like to thank my mother; she gave me a spirit! Thanks to everyone who's helped me out with the organising of this my first exhibition. Thanks to Steve for the coffee table that I painted and also for the framing. And to Megan, my lady, and her mum Margaret—everyone—as I see your faces. Anna, thanks mate, and thank you everyone for coming. Enjoy the exhibition.'

They all clapped him loudly, coming up and shaking his hands. Then all the socialising began. It was wonderful to see my big son's face glowing with pride. The girls from Allawah, Elaine and Sharon, passed out damper and cakes, while the littlies chased each other about all over the place. The atmosphere was alive and exciting. Nobby and Megan and her mother appeared with champagne, and we toasted each other, crossing our glasses, the champers goin down real well.

The keeper of the gallery came up and introduced himself, sayin, 'It's the best exhibition we've had here!' That pleased Nobby greatly. What a wonderful turnout!

Goin on nine o'clock, I left to go home to Allawah with Sharon and Elaine on the bus. Nobby told me later that after the opening he was shanghaied by friends and taken to a restaurant in Glebe, then on to the local pub where everyone carried on regardless. It had been a very successful exhibition, because Nobby had sold nearly all the paintings that were for sale on the first night.

More important though, my son had found his forté in life.

11

GUNGABULS, AGAIN!

On 15 September 1994, I had a terrible foreboding that something bad was gonna happen. I don't know why I felt this way. Nobby was with Megs and they were very happy together, in fact they had become engaged, and Nobby was in a good frame of mind.

Nobby had been staying over at Megs' place most of the time, and he only went back to his flat to pick up extra clothes and things. Problem was, he had let two of his old jail acquaintances use his flat while he wasn't there. They said they had nowhere else to stay.

I got a phone call from Macka saying that Nob was in police custody. He, Nob and Megs had gone over to the flat in Glebe to get Nob a change of clothes. While they were there, the gungies raided the place and found a phial of amphetamines. Nob tried to tell them that although the flat was his, he'd given the key to two friends who had no place to stay. The police said that if he didn't admit the amphetamines were his they'd charge his mate and his fiancée. Nob, being the kind of person he is said, yes, the drugs were his. He wanted to protect Megs, and Macka, who was dying of hepatitis. Those great friends of his that he let have his room couldn't be found anywhere. They'd been using his room as a drug drop-off place.

So my son was gone again, back to the Big House. Bail was refused. There were three charges that they'd hit him with. I was so devastated; Megs was too. So much for all dreams and plans they'd made, aye!

Macka came over to Allawah to see me before he and his family went back home to Coonabarabran. It made me cry when he said, 'This should never have happened, Ruby I couldn't help Nob in any way.'

'He should know better than to trust anyone,' I said, 'but that's just the way he is. He'll have to stay away from so-called mates that use him up like this.'

By March 1995, Nob had been incarcerated for six months at Long Bay Remand Centre. He'd been back to court a few times but remanded each time. I don't know what seemed to happen to my son because every time he was jailed he closed up shop and refused to see any of us family members. I thought maybe he's ashamed of always endin up behind bars. I don't know. But the only one he wanted to see was Megs. Besides, I was sick of runnin to cop shops and jails.

I wore the blanket (took the blame) for a mate of mine when he left something at my place in Glebe. The police was checkin him out and his mates. They must have followed his mates to my place. I'd let this mate have my keys because he had no place to stay and at that time I was practically livin at Megs' place. And one night I came home to get some clothes because I was actually goin to meet the Mayor of Randwick. That night I was pinched, cause this great mate of mine left something in my flat and the coppers were gonna arrest my lady and Macka, me mate from Coonabarabran. But I just put me hand up and said it was mine. They just let them go, and I went back to jail for eighteen months. I'd never been busted for drugs ever in my life before, and the drugs weren't mine. I felt shamed

*cause it's just not in my criminal history, drug use. Anybody
who knows me knows I don't go near that stuff.*

But when he was gonna be sentenced he asked for me to
be there in the courtroom. I went and Megs met me there.
I brought along some of my books to show to the barrister,
even the one with Nobby's art work on the cover—a
volume of the journal *Australian/Canadian Studies*.[1] It had
part of Nobby's life story in it, and I wanted to show the
judge to try and impress him that Nob was not a lost cause
after all.

We didn't get into the court till after two o'clock and
when they brought Nobby in I smiled and waved at him.
While all the prosecutor's evidence was being given, the
courtroom became like a morgue. You could hear a pin
drop. Then Megs got up and spoke on Nobby's behalf, and
Nobby's barrister spoke about his art, passing Nobby's
portfolio to the judge to look at. The judge remarked how
talented Nobby was, saying, 'I wish I had your ability to
do this kind of art work.' But then he was talking about
Nobby's record saying how bad his record was. It made
my heart sink. He gave him a twelve-month sentence, with
a further twelve months' probation on top of that. Even
while he was sentencing Nobby, the old big-wig was still
raving on about Nobby's past as far back as the children's
homes.

I was thinkin to myself: all right your judge-ship, if you
want to bring up my son's past, how about the past of all
you colonisers and invaders of our country, and the mis-
deeds that your people did to my people? Let's have a look
at some of that disastrous stuff that went down, because
that past is not finished. The effects of the past are still
present today, your worship.

The judge was still raving on about Nob while he was
being led back to the cells by two policemen. Then the

judge recognised me sitting there and said, 'I've read your books, Mrs Langford. I admire your writing.' I was so disgusted with the whiteman's so-called justice system, which we Kooris had been forced to live with for so many years now, that I stood up and said, 'You couldn't have been listening very much to what I've been writing about, Your Honour, because the only sore point in my life has been the incarceration of my son at seventeen-and-a-half for something he never did. We Kooris do not have any human rights in this country.'

He replied, 'That's not right, Mrs Langford. You do.'

I snapped back, 'While even some of my people are without fresh drinking water, and are dying of curable diseases and are the most jailed people in Australia, we do *not* have any human rights.' Then I grabbed my bag and walked out of the court room, leaving the judge with his mouth wide open.

When me and Megs left to go home we both had a good cry. We got a taxi and dropped her off at her mum's place at Balmain, then I went on alone to Allawah feeling how hopeless we Koori people have been in the white 'justice system'.

I was so disgusted about what happened that I decided to write a letter to the judge.

20 May 1995
Dear Judge ——

I'm writing this letter to you in the hope that I might enlighten you, as a member of the judiciary, about Aboriginal incarceration and its side effects of Aboriginal deaths in custody, and the effect it has on Koori people's lives.

I'll start at the beginning. We, the Aboriginal people of Australia, had our own democratic laws before the coming of the white man to our shores. We had a system where no one was excluded. There were no kings or queens. We had tribal elders. If you mucked up in tribal society, you were banished forever, and if you broke the marriage laws you were stood up in front of the tribe and spears were thrown at you until you were dead! This was our justice.

Then with what we termed the invasion in 1788, you mob came from England with your laws—the Westminster system of justice. We were forced to adopt your rules and laws, because Aboriginal spears were no match for muskets. Then in 1883, the Aborigines Protection Act was formed in New South Wales. Your people did not want my people wandering all over the place like we'd done for centuries before white man came. The first squatters fenced the land off, claiming it as their own, declaring it was *terra nullius*, empty land. Yet that was a big lie! Our indigenous people were here since time immemorial. The last carbon dating proved that our people were in this land sixty to a hundred thousand years ago. This puts an end to the other great myth that we migrated here from Asia when the sea levels were low after the last great ice age fifteen thousand years ago. We were always here you know. We come from the earth. The earth is our mother. In Aboriginal society we were animals, birds, fish, insects, and plants before we became human beings.

In your Anglo society, as the scientists say, all life forms evolved from the sea. Or some believe that your mob came from Adam and Eve, and that God created heaven and earth, working for six days and resting on the Sabbath, the seventh day. In our Dreaming, our Aboriginal Dreamtime means before creation time, when the earth was flat and empty, the great spirit forces moved over the land creating the mountains, the valleys, the rivers and streams, plants and animals, and setting down the laws and rules for Aboriginal people (the world's oldest surviving race of people) to live by. This is our Dreamtime and what it means.

When the squatters fenced the land off it placed great hardship on my people. We didn't have access to our bush tucker, and when our people took sheep or cattle because of hunger they were shot.

There were 500 tribes and 2300 dialects, but 300 Aboriginal nations died through the so-called colonisation of our lands, through introduced diseases, poisoning of waterholes and the gun, which we had no control over. Before white settlement, there were three to four hundred thousand Aboriginal people in the whole of the continent, and recent research has placed the figure nearer to the million mark. But in 1920, just over 130 years after the settlement, there were just 60 000 of us left. That will just tell you how much our people were decimated by this invasion of our lands.

In the 1800s the missions and reserves were formed and my people were rounded up like cattle and placed on them. I was born on one so I know what I'm talkin about. These places always had white managers. We had to get permission to come and go. If outside work was wanted you had to have permission from the manager. He was like a camp commandant of a Nazi prison camp. So our people were controlled way back then. And later they started to round up the half-caste kids. They didn't want them growing up tribally, because our traditional ones were classified as heathen and vermin to be cleared off the face of the earth. The half-caste kids were taken from their families and placed in the homes to be trained in servitude for white people. Only 8000 recorded cases of these stolen generations were known about, but later research has placed the number at 20 000 in NSW and 30 000 in Western Australia.

Most of the stolen children who got out of the boys' and girls' training homes don't know who they are, or where their people are, or where they come from. That's because they were denied their Aboriginality in these homes, not allowed to acknowledge their cultural heritage, or speak their tribal language, or even have visits from their parents. Conform, they were told! Conform to the white man's ways, lose all Aboriginal identity, be like white people. And then these are the people who end up in jail and are still being judged by their childhood records from the homes. So they go from the homes to the Big House—Long Bay Gaol—being charged and recharged on evidence from their childhood. No wonder we are the most jailed people in this country we once called our homelands.

We have been torn apart, split asunder, divided and quartered by the dominant culture in Australian society, through no fault of our own, only for the fact that we are Aboriginals and the first people of this land. We don't have any justice here and never have since you mob came.

Your Honour, my son served six years of a ten-year sentence for something he never did. He was incarcerated at seventeen-and-a-half because the police had to have a conviction, so he wore that charge. My people are still being brutalised in the prison and police systems in this country today. We want to know when will the punishments end?

When I went to court for his sentencing this last time, I was amazed to hear you bringing up his childhood past in a grown-up court of law. I thought that when you have been charged and served your time for a crime when you are a child, your record would not be used against you in a grown-up court. Seems unfair to me as in America, I think, if you have been free of imprisonment for eight to ten years your criminal slate is wiped clean. But apparently not so in old colonial Australia! The chains are still around my people's necks—the chains of oppression!

Your Honour, some of the recommendations of the Royal Commission into Aboriginal Deaths in Custody stated that you people—the judges, the juries, the police and prison officers, lawyers, barristers, all of you people—should know about our Aboriginal dispossession in our own country so you could be fair and non-racist when dealing with us in the courts of this land. I feel you people must know about that dispossession from our Aboriginal perspective. So please don't take offence at my attempts to educate you judiciary mob.

Ruby Langford Ginibi

I really wanted to include the judge's reply to my letter in this book, but he wouldn't give permission, so I'll just give you the gist of how Aboriginal people are portrayed in the judicial system of this country. I was very offended by some of the things he said. He didn't mean to offend me but some of his remarks and the language he used did. He addressed me by my first name in a paternalistic way as if he was a personal friend, which he is not. And every time he referred to Aboriginal people, which was on numerous occasions, he always used a small 'a', not a capital 'A'. How would he like it if I referred to him as an Australian with a small 'a'?

He returned, by postpak, my three books which I had sent to his chambers to edu-ma-cate him. It was my way of trying to open up his eyes. In his letter to me he called for tolerance from both sides, and I agree with this. But he did not believe my opinions about white people knowing little about Aboriginal dispossession.

He told me about an incident that happened twenty years ago, when an Aboriginal protester spat at his wife when they were protesting against a South African rugby team touring Australia. To that I say, he was outraged about South Africa, but what about racism in Australia? The spitting happened twenty years ago, yet he still remembers it. Now he knows how racism has affected my people who have been copping it every day, all our lives.

He told me he had travelled widely as a judge around New South Wales visiting missions and Aboriginal community centres, trying to see for himself how Aboriginal people are living. I think he really needs to broaden his horizons a bit more. We need full-on help in our organisation.

He might be a busy man but does he give practical help to my people? He wrote of having two Aboriginal women run some ideas by him after he had sentenced their brothers to jail for armed robberies. It's a shame my people have to go to these white authorities, cap in hand, to find solutions to our problems.

The judge told me I'm not being fair in my assessment of white people's ignorance and he reckoned we shouldn't take sides. If we didn't take sides, though, it'd be a bloody one-sided argument, which it often is now. He said nothing would get better with generalisations based on ignorance, to which I say yes, this I know because his mob have always been ignorant about my people.

The judge went on to say that he wasn't English but Irish, and that his people had been killed by the English and oppressed by their English laws. So we have some common ground. Why doesn't he have some more empathy and understanding towards our Aboriginal situation in this land?

The judge told me he was an atheist and didn't believe in any religion but he respected the beliefs of others. He wasn't one of the missionaries who rammed religion down our throats, but as a judge he is one of the powerbrokers who are still jailing our people according to laws that are thought to have God's blessing, God's power, and God's authority. He acts in the name of God although he doesn't believe in God.

I probably assumed all my life that white people were all the same in their thinking and morality, and the judge pulled me up on this. Sorry about this assumption of mine, your Judgeship. But is my prejudice really surprising given the treatment of Aboriginal people by white people and white courts? Like a lot of white people, I tend to get carried away and make generalisations.

The judge wrote that he respected my beliefs that my

son was innocent at seventeen-and-a-half. He said the law is human; it makes mistakes. He couldn't comment on Nobby's case as he knew nothing of its details. I would have thought that as he was sitting in judgement on Nobby's case, he would have had all the files there in front of him. They were bringing up evidence going back to Nobby's early days of juvenile incarceration.

The judge stated that class rather than race was the deciding factor on Aboriginal incarceration. To this I say he overlooks the fact that laws were made restricting Aboriginal people's lives—in every way, their movements, the taking of their children, etc.—and these laws were made for Aboriginal people only. Instead of asking why so many Aborigines are in prison, he thought the question should be: Why are so many of the socially disadvantaged people ending up in prison? To this I say, the laws of the dominant white culture were the laws of upper-class white men in England. These laws were bad for poor whites, especially women, but we Aboriginal people had double the amount of oppression because we were singled out for unfair treatment on the basis of our race as well.

The judge claimed that more whites die in prison than Aborigines, but there had been no 'white deaths in custody' inquiry. But he wasn't looking at the statistics proportionately. If white prisoners died at the same rate as Aboriginal prisoners, there would have been over 2500 deaths in the 1980s. I bet there would have been a big official inquiry into *that*!

He said that Aborigines and women are treated more favourably than white males by the courts. I say to him, if Aboriginal people are treated so leniently, why do Mick Dodson's statistics show that Aboriginal people, especially juveniles like my son when he first went to jail, are more likely to be given custodial sentences than whites for the same offence?

The judge wrote that he was ignorant of traditional Aboriginal law because it was so secret. That's not the case. Only some limited parts of it are secret. And traditional tribal law is always subordinate to white law: why else do traditional tribal people have to sing their songs and do their dances and ceremonies to prove their ownership of the land to white Native Title tribunals? If, as the judge suggested, it is inappropriate for urban Aboriginal people to be judged by traditional tribal law, how much more inappropriate is it for Aboriginal people in general to be subjected to foreign white laws?

He asked me why I despised the institution that ultimately abolished *terra nullius* and set up Mabo rights. May I remind him that the law also upheld the doctrine of *terra nullius* for over two hundred years. Even under Mabo, there's only been a handful of Aboriginal land claims that have succeeded. And now, under John Howard's ten-point plan, his answer to the High Court's Wik judgement, white law will give some rights to pastoralists and miners, and convert leasehold to an effective freehold title. We have been dispossessed for a second time—no involvement with Koori people, only Senator Harradine and John Howard. This is no democracy we live in when the highest courts in the land give us Mabo and Wik and then, with a stroke of the pen, John Howard and Senator Harradine throw out all our Koori rights to land. It's always been the miners and pastoralists who have had the wealth from the land. These aren't little Ozzie battlers (like my mob); they're some of the richest people in Australia, including members of Howard's own cabinet.

With Nobby's dealings with the legal processes and courts and these concerns dealing with incarceration of our people, Nobby and I feel that all these people should be educated about what our dispossession in our own land has done to us, the stealing of our kids, the forced total denial of our history, and the non-acknowledgement of our Aboriginal heritage. He feels that these people in the legal processes like judges, lawyers, police, and prison officers have very warped ideas about Aboriginal people. There should be educational workshops provided to let them learn from what it's like from an Aboriginal perspective so they can be less racist in their attitudes and findings towards us! And this needs to be taught to all personnel dealing with incarceration because Nobby says they know 'fuck all' about us which causes them to oppress us even more!

At least the judge ordered Nobby to be sent to Kirconnell Prison out past Lithgow to be close to family access. But he was shanghaied to Junee Prison instead, a private one right down near the Victorian border. He was frantic. No work. No art. Nothing. No wonder some people hang themselves. It must be torture for them. I had to get the Aboriginal Deaths in Custody Watch Committee to push for him to go back to Kirconnell. When Nobby was eventually transferred, Megs moved up to the Blue Mountains to be near him for visiting. They were planning to get married when Nobby was released.

12

THE WEDDING

Nobby was discharged from Kirconnell Prison on 13 March 1996, and he and Megs decided to get married. Owing to the continual incarceration, Nobby hadn't been around when most of my other children got married. So when he and Megs decided on 18 May for their wedding, I burst out laughin sayin, 'Boy, you sure are keepin the wedding dates in the family, son. I've only got two of you boys left, aye, and ya baby brother Jeffery got married to Michelle on 19 May. So you'll be able to celebrate together.'

On the day Nobby was released from Kirconnell, Megs and her mother organised everything. I was happy to see he was going to settle down. He and Megs were ideally suited, and looked like they were made for each other. The wedding invites said

Philip & Margaret Mitchell
request the pleasure of the company of
Ruby Langford Ginibi
at the marriage of their daughter Megan Louise,
to Nobby Langford
on the 18th May, 1996 at 3.30 pm,
at 'Tallowood',
76 Ashtons Road, Grose Wold (map enclosed)

followed by a reception
at 4.45 pm at the Windsor Function Centre,
Cnr Dight & Macquarie Streets, Windsor.

Time seemed to go so quickly after the invitations went
out. Nobby was painting, and had also gone back to being
a part-time courier to help out with expenses. There was
much rushin around by Megs, and Nobby gettin anxious
I suppose.

The day of the wedding arrived, but it was drizzly rain
and I was hoping it would stay fine for this great day in
the life of my son and future daughter-in-law. I'd asked
permission for Mum Joyce to stay overnight at Allawah,
and we would be travelling to the ceremony with Irina
Dunn (not a relative of the bride, but the co-ordinator of
Rozelle Writers' Centre), who had launched my third book
and was a good friend of mine. She'd had Nobby's paintings of me and Max Silva hanging at the Writers' Centre
to promote his art work.

By the time I got dressed it was nearly time for Irina
to arrive. Nobby had asked me to wear our colours and I
didn't want to disappoint him, so I had my black warm
poncho, and red dress, with my trade-mark hat, with all
my Koori badges and ribbons, and black stockings and
shoes, and a black handbag. Mum was dressed in a nice
fawn-coloured suit. We sat out on the front verandah of
Allawah, and pretty soon Irina showed up and it started
to rain, so we took an umbrella with us.

Irina had also brought my nephew Brad Webb with her
as co-pilot, cause she didn't know the way out to Richmond. We were soon on our way towards the expressway
and then on to Penrith.

We were hardly talking because the rain made us
miserable. Brad was glancing at me and watching his
watch. It made me all the more anxious about the time.

But soon we were in Richmond, then going left to find Grose Wold Road. It was now three o'clock, and we turned into the driveway of 'Tallowood' as all the other cars were coming in. Just as we got out, the car of the groom and his attendants drove in and I poked my tongue out at them. Me and Mum Joyce hurried off to the toilet, in this beautiful two-storey place. Everyone was gathered on the verandah out of the showery rain that was falling. I glanced at my two sons, Jeffery and Nobby. They scrubbed up pretty well. The best man, Macka, looked real deadly too. Me and Mum Joyce came around to the back verandah near the pergola where the wedding was gonna take place. When the rain stopped, chairs were set out in front of the pergola. Margaret, the bride's mother, and June, the marriage celebrant, guided me and Mum Joyce to sit and wait for the bride's arrival.

I looked at my biggest son, and could see he was gettin panicky. 'Get me a glass of water, Macka. My mouth is real dry,' he croaked. We laughed at his nervousness, me and Mum Joyce, chucklin to ourselves. As we waited, I looked around the pergola. Beautiful slipper orchids were blooming, bright yellow ones, and a variety of other creepers and plants, which made this a special place to be married in.

Nobby was watching his watch. So was everybody else. The bride was late—half an hour late. But it was usual for the bride to be late, aye? Then everyone was asking where was the dancer, Matthew Doyle, who was gonna play the bride and groom onto the pergola with the didge and clap sticks instead of the usual 'Here Comes the Bride' played by an organist. I thought this was a wonderful cultural acknowledgement for our people. Reconciliation had begun already.

Then into the driveway came the wedding car with the bride, and while the celebrant arranged Nobby, Jeffery, and

Macka, the stillness was shattered by the guttural sounds of the didgeridoo. And there was my daughter Ellen accompanying Matthew with the clap sticks—clack, clack, clack. The sounds echoed all around the valley.

Then the bridesmaids, two of them, looking lovely, sashayed up and stood next to the groomsmen on the pergola. Next came the beautiful bride with her Dad, Philip, dressed in his officer's uniform. He'd been a pilot, one of the Red Arrows, a famous top gun. Now he led his daughter up and put her hands in my son's hands.

And the ceremony began. By then I was misty eyed, and so was Mum Joyce. We had a ringside seat, right on the pergola, along with the wedding group. As the words were said over these two handsome people, I was thinkin it sure took my son a long time to take this big step. I guess he thought everyone in the family were leaving him for dead, as they all had established families of their own.

When the ceremony was over, Matthew put a tape on and entertained the audience with our traditional dancing. Ellen was still doing a good job on the clap sticks. She looked beautiful in her blue velvet dress, and hair done up. The photos were being taken, all the immediate family first, then everyone else. The whole ceremony was videoed too. It's a good way of keeping happy memories, aye.

The champagne was flowing while we waited for everyone else to leave for the reception. I had to travel in a wedding car, so they put me into a Daimler—huge it was! At the convention centre, everyone else was upstairs waiting for the wedding group. I hobbled up the stairs and sat down with all my family—Shellie, Davey-boy, Jaymi, and Debbie-Joe. They'd missed the wedding as they'd gotten lost! So they just came straight to the reception.

Then my name was called out and an usher took me to my seat at the wedding table. They all clapped me, then the wedding group, and finally the bride and groom came in to tremendous applause. We were served first then the others helped themselves to a smorgasbord of beautiful food. A wonderful time was had by all. After eating, everyone was up boogyin. They even played Kenny Rogers singing 'Ruby, Don't Take Your Love To Town'. All my mob were up dancing and singin it to me, and I called out to them, 'If I didn't take my love to town, you mob wouldn't be here!' After all the formalities were over and it was time to go, we all gathered in the foyer. They seated me in a big chair, while the bride threw her bouquet. It was caught by the best man's little daughter. Then the groom had to remove the bride's garter with his teeth. The crowd were clappin and cheering Nobby on. Then everyone formed a big circle, and the bride went one way while the groom went the other, saying goodbye to family and friends. Then the last part of the guests formed a guard of honour with hands held high so the happy couple could run through, goin out the door to get into their bright yellow hot rod that would take them to their motel for the night.

Rumour has it that me and Megs' cultural wedding was the talk of the town. We had Matthew Doyle, the famous dancer and didgeridoo player. He gave my wife's hand to me in marriage in our traditional way. And he danced, and played the didgeridoo while Ellen my sister played the clap sticks. It was just an absolutely beautiful day. My brother was dancing, my sisters too. Thank the good spirit that the rain held off as it was an overcast day.

Before they left, I came out front, along with all the others waving them goodbye, and, as they were getting into the car, something distracted me and made me look on the top of the car. I was struck dumb! There was a circle of faces I knew very well! The spirits of John Pat, Robert Walker, Charlie Michaels, Eddie Murray, David Gundy, and Daniel

Yock! They were callin out to Nobby, sayin, 'On ya brother. You survived the brutal jails. We didn't make it. Long life and much happiness to you and your lady. Go in peace, and live for all of us!'

And then Nobby looked up and waved, and I knew he's seen them too!

Since this is my son Nobby's life story and it's about Aboriginal deaths in custody too, I think it's relevant that he has the last word with this poem he wrote in Long Bay Gaol in 1988 titled, 'The Bicentennial'.

'The Bicentennial'
Nobby Langford

It isn't really that long ago, it seems as yesterday,
When Captain Cook and his whitemen set foot on
Botany Bay. Please pause a moment and sincerely
observe, the mess our country is in today.
It's nineteen eighty-eight, early September, What justice
to the black man do we render?
After all, it's been two hundred years of savage
beatings, shame, blood and tears
For this nation of black people they called savages!
In their sadistic brutal murders, our cause is vindicated;
The gentry, noses in the air, the victims left
emancipated.
They stole our land, treating us despicably,
And when we tried to talk to them amicably,
Our numbers by the thousands were killed and
decimated.
When by sons of 'CONVICTS' our lives were violated,
Our women raped and our children taken into slavery,
We did not remonstrate, but suffered silently, bravely.
The whiteman, never satisfied, did rape and plunder.

Our families torn apart, the love of kin was split
asunder!
If this wasn't quite enough to be so denigrated,
Land owners, cattlemen, and graziers—their hate never
abated.
If any blackman dared to complain, he was beaten or
strangulated.
All justice was ignored, no laws against this horror
formulated.
They want to give us back some of our land,
So white Australians can hide their shame.
Deep under their skin lies hate and discrimination.
They know they're guilty of genocide, human
extermination!
Today in this, the third century,
Our cries for freedom are muffled by white majority,
And our young men are framed and hung by the
authorities
Whose biased laws are one huge travesty.
The time is ripe to stand up and be counted,
So our cries are heard, and all the obstacles
surmounted. You better listen whiteman, I tell you from
my heart:
We have to live together, at the same time apart!

NOTES

PREFACE

Australian Bureau of Statistics, Census 1991, 1994.

Crawford F., 'Jalinardi Ways—Whitefellas Working in Aboriginal Communities', Curtin University of Technology, 1989.

Dagger D., 'Persons in Juvenile Corrective Institutions', Australian Institute of Criminology, ed. S. Mukherjee, no. 66, table 9.

Interview with P. Reberger, Executive Director, Minda Juvenile Justice Centre, September 1995.

CHAPTER 1

1. From the report on the Stolen Generation, *Bringing Them Home* April 1997.

CHAPTER 4

1. P. O'Shane, *Aboriginal and Islander Health Worker Journal*, vol. 19, May/June 1995, p. 28.

2. *Paperbark—A Collection of Black Australian Writings*, ed. Jack Davis et al., University of Queensland Press, 1990, p. 149.

CHAPTER 6

1. D. Horton (ed.), 'Black deaths in custody' in *The Encyclopaedia of Aboriginal Australia*, Vol. 1, A–L, Aboriginal Studies Press, for Aboriginal and Torres Strait Islander Studies, Canberra, 1994, p. 439.
2. John O'Sullivan, *Mounted Police in NSW*, Rigby, Adelaide, 1979.
3. Anti-Discrimination Board, *Study of Street Offences by Aborigines*, 1982, pp. 117, 123.
4.–6. Case file material from the Aboriginal Legal Service.
7. Robert Walker, 'Solitary Confinement' in *Up, Not Down, Mate! Thoughts from a Prison Cell*, Adelaide, 1987.
8.–11. Case file material from the Aboriginal Legal Service.
12. Graeme Dixon, 'Battle Heroes' in *Holocaust Island*, University of Queensland Press, 1990.

CHAPTER 9

1. For photos and information about Sam Anderson, see Graham Smith, *How It Seemed*, The Northern Star, Lismore, 1985.
2. Aboriginal legends found in Bill Magee, *The Shadow of Mount Lindesay*, Warwick Newspaper Pty Ltd, Warwick, 1987.

CHAPTER 11

1. Nobby's artwork was featured on the cover of *Australian/Canadian Studies*, vol. 11, nos 1 and 2, 1993.